Praise for *The Creation Frequency*

"In this groundbreaking book, Mike Murphy provides a simple yet potent method to supercharge your vision and awareness by teaching you how to open to greater love, creativity, inspiration, and the power to manifest what is truly meaningful."

— **Marcia Wieder**, CEO of Dream University

"Mike Murphy's book is a rare coming together of the inspirational and the practical. The tools to truly change your life are here. Mike's journey from the troubled young man that he was to the wise and compassionate man that he is will move you to trust the power of love if you let it."

— **Dale Borglum**, executive director of the Living/Dying Project

"Fascinating! Mike Murphy weaves a masterpiece that melds sound and prolific research with that which is elusively spiritual and often neglected as subjective and trivial. The research is thorough and clearly makes the reader consider the reality of the metaphysical in everyday living. *The Creation Frequency* is not just theory. It is a pragmatic blueprint for every seeker to systematically pursue abundance and self-actualization in their life. The text is so captivating that I finished reading it in one sitting."

— **Reggie Chandra**, I

T012594З

Praise for *Love Unfiltered* by Mike Murphy

"*Love Unfiltered* is a story about a powerful love between two people, as well as a story about how universal love can transcend time, borders, and differences. What a beautiful reminder that we are all here simply to love."

— **Marci Shimoff,** *New York Times*–bestselling author
of *Happy for No Reason*

"I remember the first time I met Mike Murphy. I thought to myself, 'This guy has an enormous heart.' Since then that heart has been broken, and the story in these pages is that gripping story. But with a broken heart he is more generous than ever, especially with his encouragement of others. This book will make you rethink your life in a profound way."

— **Matthew Kelly,** *New York Times*–bestselling author
of *The Rhythm of Life*

THE
CREATION
FREQUENCY

Also by Mike Murphy

Love Unfiltered:
Tear Down Your Walls,
Open Your Heart,
Live Your Life On Purpose

THE CREATION FREQUENCY

Tune In to the Power of the Universe
to Manifest the Life of Your Dreams

MIKE MURPHY

New World Library
Novato, California

New World Library
14 Pamaron Way
Novato, California 94949

Text design by Tona Pearce Myers

Library of Congress Cataloging-in-Publication data is available.

First printing, May 2018
ISBN 978-1-60868-554-7
Ebook ISBN 978-1-60868-555-4
Printed in Canada on 100% postconsumer-waste recycled paper

New World Library is proud to be a Gold Certified Environmentally Responsible Publisher. Publisher certification awarded by Green Press Initiative. www.greenpressinitiative.org

10   9   8   7   6   5   4   3   2

In memory of Douglas Fitzgerald,
a.k.a. the mystery man —
thank you.
You gave me the tools to create the most wonderful life.

And dedicated to my dad, Bob Murphy,
who taught me the ultimate success principle:
"If you are going to do something,
give it all that you have, or don't do it!"
Love you, Dad.

CONTENTS

A NOTE TO THE READER

In the pages of this book, I will be teaching you a process that I have developed based upon one that was taught to me by a mysterious stranger more than three decades ago. During the process of writing this book, I was able to connect with the family of this man, who recently passed away, and to gain access to some of his writings. I have taken the liberty of supplementing my limited memories of our conversations with short passages from his writings, to give my readers a fuller sense of this unusual man than I personally could recall. With this exception, all the facts of my stories are told exactly as they occurred, including the miraculous results that I achieved by following the process he taught me.

FOREWORD

For more than three decades, I've been teaching people how to manifest their goals, dreams, and desires. When I met Mike Murphy, I was immediately struck by his inspirational story of putting the law of attraction into practice. This man went from being divorced, in debt, and abusing drink and drugs to being a successful entrepreneur, making millions of dollars, and creating a beautiful life for himself and his family. He went from loneliness to extraordinary love. He went from being in desperate need of help himself to being able to contribute and help others through charitable work. He went from being lost and aimless to living his life on purpose. And he did all of this through applying the essential principles of the law of attraction.

The principles Mike shares in this book are steps anyone can take to create the life of their dreams. Unlike many books on manifestation, *The Creation Frequency* is full of very practical advice and offers a clear, specific process you can use to ensure success.

As I have often said, the law of attraction comes down

to three steps: Ask, believe, and receive. Asking means being clear about what you want — writing down and visualizing your goals, dreams, and desires in as much detail as possible. Believing means creating a state of positive expectation that your goals are attainable and achievable. Receiving, the final step, might sound like the passive part, the moment when you sit back and watch it all show up. What Mike understands and shares in this book is that being ready to receive is not passive at all.

Receiving takes a lot of work. Imagine that you ordered a package, and UPS shows up to deliver it, but your mailbox is too small to let it in. You need to expand the size of the mailbox. And the size of the mailbox is a metaphor for the frequency of the vibrations you are putting out into the Universe.

Ultimately, as Mike shares in these pages, everything is made up of energy, which is vibrating at different frequencies. Your thoughts and emotions each vibrate at a specific frequency. Receiving is the stage at which most people stumble because they don't realize that they are actually sending out negative vibrations into the Universe that push away the very things they want to attract.

In order to attract what you want, you have to create a vibrational match for it within yourself. When you are in a state of love, joy, generosity, gratitude, and expansiveness, you are more likely to attract things into your life that generate more love, joy, generosity, gratitude, and expansiveness.

In my experience, love is the highest frequency, and

it is the key to manifestation — not just in the realm of relationships, but in business, finance, health, and every other arena of life. Love is like a diamond with many facets. It can take the form of joy, of peace, of excitement, or of purpose. As Mike explains beautifully in this book, love is ultimately the energy that makes manifestation possible.

Mike Murphy is a beautiful man with a big heart, and his own example of learning to work with the power of love is both inspirational and empowering. *The Creation Frequency* gives you the tools to manifest everything you desire — in your relationships, your businesses, your bank accounts, your health, and your contributions to others. Read these pages, and then go out and create the life of your dreams!

— **Jack Canfield,** author of *The Success Principles*™ and *Jack Canfield's Key to Living the Law of Attraction*

PREFACE

You are holding a real gem of a book in your hands right now. It's simple, straightforward, and honest, and it encapsulates a huge amount of truth in relatively few pages. Many books have been written about creating or materializing the "stuff of your life," and some make it seem so complicated! Actually, it's much easier than our left brain would have us think. Mike Murphy has lived the process so effectively that he's truly earned the right to be called an expert on the subject.

I've known Mike for a number of years, and I've always been impressed by how his devilish, rebellious early life led him to become so open-minded, caring, and visionary. He set to work achieving his desires without struggle, and he has demonstrated how materializing visions is a normal function of consciousness — of using both the left and right brain and the body consciousness. Mike has been successful in the physical world and equally so in the nonphysical world of feeling and thought, of energy and attention. He is a humble and worthy teacher for this material, and a clear communicator to boot.

I agree with Mike totally: A big part of the secret to materializing your visions is learning how to get to the deep place, your soul's home frequency, where your truest desires abide. Not all those deep desires are lofty, humanitarian, and spiritual in nature. To want to own a house, or have enough healthy food, or an inspiring view, or nice clothes, or a new car — these might be necessary to help you relax and feel good about yourself so you can more easily access your true desires. When the debilitating distractions and stressors are minimized, you become more transparent, and your deep desires fall through the clarity into your conscious mind.

When (1) your left brain chooses to live in the feeling state you love, and (2) your actions and accomplishments come from and perpetuate that state, you end up being in alignment with your soul and the universal laws. When that happens, you can materialize anything — and you realize there are endless choices that don't necessarily have to follow some logical projected path forward. You are not limited to what has happened to you historically; you're in the vast present moment, where something new can appear out of the blue. And there is no special kind of grandiose materialization that will make you better than others. Creating something small is as joyful as creating something large and complex. It is your ability to work with your intuition and your right-brain attention that opens you to the direct experience of life's unlimited nature — and of your own unlimited capabilities.

Another big part of materializing your visions is

developing trust — that is, trust in you-the-soul's plan for you-the-personality's life, in the power of the collective consciousness and the flow to bring the "just right" next thing, in your ability to notice what you need to notice and make it meaningful in an accurate way, and in the deep inner goodness of all people and their desire to cocreate and help one another evolve. It is really your undivided attention to a reality you want to experience that draws it toward you — or more accurately, allows it to emerge out of the field of energy around you with great synchronicity and perfection. When you love the desire, it loves you. When you keep your attention on the experience of the vision and feel into it with your senses, it suddenly shows up in your field, no willpower required.

Mike and I were talking the other day about how after you start learning this way of materializing desires, the idea of hard work and effort fades, to be replaced by a sense of playing or *just waiting*. You begin to have an unimpeachable faith in your own self and the mechanics of life, in other people and perfect timing, and in your intuition and instinct about stepping into an action without planning to do it first. The right thoughts, resources, choices, and higher-level desires show up right as you realize you want them. Life takes on a real synchromesh quality.

You realize that when you think the world is physical and solid, life seems difficult, and you see yourself as separate from what you want. But when you move into the nonphysical inner realms via meditation, intuition, or mindfulness, you realize the physical world is really made of energy functioning at various frequencies, all interpenetrating, and the energy shapes itself into form according to your consciousness. You experience how you are energy living in a field of energy with no barriers separating anything. I like what Mike says about the Universe being so sensitive to congruency, alignment, and attunement. What you want is already inside your field at a slightly different vibration. Match your frequency to that of your desire, and it can appear out of your field.

There is no shortage of resources, and no shortage of ideas and possibilities. You really can develop the skill of materializing what you want and dematerializing what you don't need anymore. Just think what your life could be like without doubt and worry! Just imagine how fast you could evolve and improve your consciousness and character when you have what you need, and know that what materializes *is* what you need! The times we're living in today, with the ongoing acceleration of the Earth's vibration, are ripe for this higher-frequency understanding and new, more frictionless experience. So, I encourage you to dive in to the simple process outlined here in *The Creation Frequency* — and see what happens! See what you can do!

— **Penney Peirce,** bestselling author of *Frequency*

Prologue

THE MYSTERY MAN

In just seven weeks, I will teach you how to turn your life around and get everything you ever wanted.

If a complete stranger made that promise to you, would you believe him? I did, several decades ago, and it was the most important decision I've ever made. I followed the instructions that stranger gave me — the same method you'll learn in this book — and every one of my dreams came true. Now, I'm promising you the same. If you choose to believe me, you won't regret it.

No matter where you are in life right now, I'm here to show you how you can have everything you ever wanted — and more. If you feel like everything's going in the wrong direction, take a deep breath and stop. I've been there. It feels like being sucked down a drain with nothing to grab hold of. But this is the moment you can turn it all around.

It doesn't matter how tough things seem, how badly

you've messed up, how many bridges you've burned or hearts you've broken, including your own. It's not too late to repair the damage and succeed beyond your wildest dreams. No matter where you are coming from, what mistakes you have made, how you have failed or stumbled on your path, you will not find judgment from me in these pages. I have known the path of fear and guilt and regret. And I have been blessed with the opportunity to turn it all around — to turn fear into love, guilt into gratitude, regret into hope. That's the opportunity I want to offer you, too.

Maybe you're thinking, "My life's not all that bad." But is it everything it could be? If you're flatlining, not really going anywhere, I can show you how to break out of the numbness and let the energy of love propel you forward into possibilities you've never allowed yourself to consider. If your life has been pretty good up until now — if you've been blessed with a supportive family, a good education, and some degree of success — then I will simply show you how to accelerate your journey. And if you've been successful beyond your wildest dreams, but find yourself still feeling like something is missing, I can help you to discover the secret that will make all of it meaningful.

I've come to understand that there is an unimaginable power within each and every one of us. For some, this may seem like only a tiny, flickering flame, almost snuffed out by the negativity in the world and the limiting beliefs in our minds. But my goal in this book is to fan this flame, to make it bright and strong and powerful so that it radiates through you in everything you do. I'd like to share my story with you because if I can get there from where I was, you can get there from here, whatever "here" looks like for you.

In one of our family albums, there is a photo of me, one year old, with a bottle of beer wedged between my chubby knees and a cigarette hanging out of my mouth. I'm sure it was just a joke on my parents' part, but unfortunately it was prescient. I started drinking in eighth grade, spent my teenage years in and out of jail, and was kicked out of three schools. Between the ages of sixteen and eighteen, I survived eight car accidents, all of them alcohol-related.

I was not the first in my family to have a drinking problem. My dad's parents were both alcoholics, and he was made a ward of the state of California at the age of thirteen. Sure enough, he grew up to become an alcoholic himself, and my mother, although sweet and loving, was unable to do anything but support his habit.

At the age of fourteen, I ran away from home, traveling from Cincinnati, Ohio, to Lexington, Kentucky, with just a few dollars in my pocket. I stayed in Lexington a few weeks before a kind priest helped me to find my way home. That was the first of a number of attempts to leave it all behind.

In my early twenties, I married Lisa, my teenage sweetheart. This drunken, spur-of-the-moment decision on my part threw together two lost and lonely young people who didn't really know themselves or each other that well. I was a terrible husband — unfaithful, eventually unemployed, and fast adopting my father's worst habits, as I drank and took drugs to dull my guilt over the disaster I was making of my marriage. In the midst of this chaos, Lisa became pregnant.

When my daughter, Michelle, was just two months old, I looked at myself in the mirror and was overwhelmed by shame and humiliation at what a loser I'd become, and the fact that everyone knew it. So I ran away from it all, just as I had as a teenager and have many times since. Only this time, Lisa had had enough. When I called her after a week of partying, she refused to take me back.

Driving aimlessly through town, I ended up at the church where we had gotten married. I wasn't a believer, but I was so desperate that I stumbled up the steps, only to find the door locked. So I sat out on those steps and I demanded that if God was real, he should manifest right there — then, and only then, would I believe, and I would change my ways. Nothing happened. But by the grace of God, the next day I found myself in an AA meeting, and for the first time in months, I felt a stirring of hope.

By the spring of 1983, I was divorced and felt like I was dying inside, although I would never admit that to anyone. I made a resolution to turn my life around, whatever it took, but I honestly didn't know if I could survive the pain in the meantime. I put on a tough face, got a job waiting tables, and dutifully fulfilled my child-support obligations. I joined a program and stopped drinking. I started reading every self-help book I could get my hands on. But the noose around my heart grew tighter and tighter the harder I tried to break through. I was living in a constant state of fear and depression. In hindsight, I think I was experiencing the accumulated pain of all my childhood wounds, but most immediately, the source of my anguish was my separation from my wife and infant daughter.

It was all my fault. That was the worst part. I had created this mess, and now I had to survive long enough to fix it. At one of my lowest moments, a good friend offered to introduce me to a man he thought could help. He scribbled an address on a piece of paper.

So it was that I found myself driving my 1971 Ford Pinto through a nondescript suburban neighborhood. Although it was a cold and rainy northern California day, I had to keep the car window open because the driver's door had been damaged and would not stay closed unless I drove with one arm holding it shut from the outside. Thus, with one wet arm and wildly disheveled hair, I pulled up outside the modest home of this mystery man.

My friend had told me that this man could help me, but it would cost me $50 an hour, an awful lot of money to me at the time. I barely scraped by on the $2,000 a month I made waiting tables in two different restaurants, and I was $40,000 in debt. But I was desperate, so I took a deep breath, scraped my wet hair off my face, and rang the doorbell.

A middle-aged guy answered the door, shook my hand, and introduced himself. I'm sure he told me his name, but strangely, for decades afterward I could not recall it, and so I always thought of him as the "mystery man." What I do recall was the feeling I got when I first laid eyes on him. My heart sank. I'd been hoping for a white-bearded wise man or an exotic-looking mystic like those I'd read about in my self-help books. This guy certainly didn't look like a miracle worker — he looked more like a schoolteacher or an accountant. He invited me into his kitchen and offered me a cup of coffee. Taking a seat opposite me, he sat quietly for a moment, and then, in a soft but surprisingly commanding voice, he made a proposal:

"Here's how it's going to work. We'll meet one hour a week for seven weeks. Between our meetings, I'll expect you to do just a little work to prepare for the next. In the seventh week, you will receive a gift that will forever change your life."

Shrinking back in my seat, all I could think about was seven times fifty — $350 that I didn't have. I also noted the simplicity of the small house, with its well-worn furniture and unremarkable location, which did not give me much confidence in this man's ability to materialize anything. It all just seemed a bit far-fetched.

I must have looked unconvinced because he suddenly pushed back his chair, stood up, and leaned across the table, so close that his face was almost touching mine. "You do this and you will get everything you want!"

His intensity took me aback, but something in his demeanor was compelling. Maybe this unassuming mystery man really did know the secret to getting my life back on track. One thing I knew for sure was that it couldn't get much worse. And I had nowhere else to turn.

As I sat there trying to decide if this was crazy or if it just might work, I remembered how one of the inspirational authors I'd been reading said that when you spend money on your mind, it is not an expense but an investment. No one had ever invested in my mind, so I figured I'd take a chance and see if it paid off. Besides, I told myself, if I didn't like the first week, I wouldn't return, so I would only be down $50. Deep down, however, I knew that this wasn't really about my mind. It was about the unrelenting pain in my heart. I scribbled out a check.

1

Why You're Not Already Living the Life of Your Dreams

WEEK ONE

What we are today comes from our thoughts of yesterday,
and our present thoughts build our life of tomorrow:
our life is the creation of our mind.

— The Buddha, from the Dhammapada

"Who are you? Who are you *really*? Are you living as your best and highest self?"

The mystery man had folded my check and put it in his pocket, and he was now interrogating me with a series of questions I didn't know how to begin to answer.

"Why are you here?" he demanded. "Why are you not living the life of your dreams?" As I fumbled for words, his expression softened.

"If you can't answer these questions, it's not your fault. Most of us fall far short of fulfilling our potential, and we don't even realize it. We've been born into a world and a system that programs us to settle for much less than we are capable of. We'll come back to those questions in a moment, but first let me ask you this: Are you ready to finally create the life you want? Are you ready to take back your power and become the author of your own destiny?"

Now that was a question I could answer. "Yes," I declared. "I'm ready."

"Good," he replied. "So you no longer want to keep creating the life you're living?"

Want? This miserable existence was the last thing I'd ever wanted, and I told him so.

He was quiet for a moment, then he looked me straight in the eye and said, "Look, I understand that you don't like your life. But here's what you need to understand: Whether you like it or not, you've created the life you are currently living — or more accurately, you've cocreated it with the Universe. And before you can have the life you want, you need to take responsibility for how you ended up where you are, and why."

I must have looked taken aback at his statement because he quickly assured me, "I'm not trying to blame you for the difficult circumstances you may find yourself in, or dismiss all your suffering as being self-created. But I am asking you to consider that you may be more powerful than you realize. You are already a creator, whether you know it or not. Your every thought, feeling, and belief, including those you are not even aware of, carries a vibration out into the Universe, and those vibrations shape the world around you."

So began my initiation into the secrets of creation. What the mystery man told me, as I sat in his kitchen that day, is that the entire Universe is made not of matter but of energy. It may look and feel solid — the chair you're sitting in, this book in your hands, the ground beneath your feet. But in fact, although you might not be able to see it, everything is vibrating, including you. Scientists since Einstein have confirmed this fact, as I have learned in my extensive reading over the years since meeting the mystery man.

Back in those days, I simply took in what he said and followed the instructions he gave me. More than three decades later, they remain the foundation of the way I create my own life and the methods I'll be teaching you in this book. But I've also done my own research, reading every book about manifestation I could get my hands on and finding a wealth of science, mysticism, and practical guidance that supports this approach and explains why it is so extraordinarily powerful. What you'll learn in these pages began with those kitchen-table conversations, but it has been enhanced by the addition of science that was not available thirty years ago, and it has been refined through years of practice and experimentation.

The Law of Attraction

Every single thing in the Universe is vibrating at a particular frequency. Your thoughts and feelings, including everything in your subconscious, are transmitting a particular vibration out into the Universe, and those vibrations shape the life you are living. This is simply how the Universe works. The good news is that once you understand how the Universe works, you have the power to get the Universe to work for you! If you're feeling stuck, unfulfilled, or dissatisfied with your life, the answer lies in raising your personal vibration to that perfect pitch where your intentions and desires resonate with the intentions and desires of the Universe.

I call this the Creation Frequency. The Creation Frequency is that sweet spot where you are "in tune" with life. When you tap into this frequency, you reclaim the creative power that is your birthright. You will find yourself able to work in partnership with the Universe to manifest the life of your dreams.

If everything in the Universe is energy, then the "things" we want are less like solid objects and more like currents of energy that we need to learn how to redirect toward ourselves. How do we direct energy? We create intention. And we create intention through the vibrations of our desires and our thoughts. What we focus on becomes our reality. As the saying goes, "Where attention goes, energy flows." Prentice Mulford, a contemporary of Emerson, wrote that our thoughts are "the unseen magnet, ever attracting its correspondence in things seen and tangible."[1]

This principle is commonly known today as "the law of attraction," but it's been around for hundreds, if not thousands, of years. From early sages like the Buddha and Lao-tzu to contemporary self-help books and movies like *The Secret*, it's been a perennial teaching that has captivated the human imagination. Even the Bible tells us, "What things soever ye desire, when ye pray, believe that ye receive them, and ye shall have them" (Mark 11:24). The sentiment was echoed centuries later in less religious terms by motivational pioneers like Ernest Holmes, author of *The Science of Mind*, and Napoleon Hill, author of *Think and Grow Rich*, who wrote, "Whatever the mind of man can conceive and believe, it can achieve." Many other great teachers and thinkers followed in their footsteps. One of my favorite contemporary systems is *A Course in Miracles*. My friend Jack Canfield, creator of the Chicken Soup for the Soul series, states the principle simply and unequivocally: "The Law of Attraction says that you will attract into your life whatever you focus on."[2]

Given the enduring popularity of this idea, you'd think we'd all be happily living idyllic lives, and there'd be no need for yet another book on how to become a creator. The secret is out. Search for "law of attraction" on Google and you will find hundreds of thousands of websites, books, courses, and so on with slogans like the following:

"Change your mind, change your life."
"Thoughts become things."
"You are what you believe yourself to be."
"Once you make a decision, the Universe conspires to make it happen."
"What you put out is what you get back."

I'd agree with most of these sentiments, at least in principle. But, clearly, it's not that simple. Too many of us — even those who've read all the self-help books, been to the seminars, and practiced the techniques — are still feeling dissatisfied and unfulfilled. Every day, I meet people, young and old, with that familiar look of longing in their eyes. Sometimes it's a powerful yearning, undimmed by life's challenges. Other times it's barely perceptible, almost extinguished by disappointment and despair. Very few people I meet seem to be truly happy and fulfilled.

According to experts, that's not surprising. Polls consistently show that the majority of us do not feel happy or satisfied with our lives. The most recent Harris Poll Happiness Index found that less than one-third of Americans report being "very happy" — a number that has been declining since the survey began in 2008.[3] Despite our ever-increasing connectedness via the internet, many of us paradoxically feel more isolated than we've ever been, with a recent AARP survey finding that 35 percent of Americans over forty-five are "chronically lonely."[4] And the rate of antidepressant use has skyrocketed over the past couple of decades, with government statisticians saying that one in every ten American teens or adults takes an antidepressant, and one in four women in their forties and fifties.[5] Clearly, the path to happiness is not as simple as thinking a few more positive thoughts. In fact, I think we need to change our focus from seeking "happiness" to seeking fulfillment or contentment. These are deeper states of alignment and congruency, not just passing feelings.

Three Keys to Manifestation

I'm not trying to dismiss all the books, courses, movies, and professionals out there who claim they can teach you how to turn your life around and attract the love, the wealth, the success, or the happiness that you long for. Some of their methods may be effective, and their fundamental premises are generally sound. Like them, I am a firm believer that our destiny is in our own hands and that we each have the power to cocreate a life of fulfillment and meaning, no matter where we come from. But I also know that this is not a quick-fix problem that can be solved by some magical secret.

Based on what the mystery man taught me, and my study of numerous other approaches, I believe that three essential elements need to be included for effective manifestation. The reason many "law of attraction" teachings and techniques fall short of changing people's lives in sustainable and measurable ways is that they fail to embrace *all three* elements. I am convinced that all three of these factors need to be addressed in order for each of us to become a powerful creator.

1. Digging Deep

Teachings on manifestation sometimes fail to dig deep enough into the subconscious roots of our current patterns of creation. If we don't effectively unearth the hidden beliefs, habits, and behavior patterns that may be blocking our ability to cocreate, including the cultural programming we've absorbed from the world around us, we'll constantly be working against ourselves. You can't transform what you can't see. And just as the subconscious mind can be the source of our biggest obstacles, it's also the source of our greatest creative power. Simply encouraging people to "think more positive thoughts" only engages the conscious mind. To become an effective creator, we need to find ways to imprint new patterns and desires into the subconscious mind. In this book, I will guide you into a new and empowered relationship with what lies beneath the surface of your everyday awareness.

2. Getting Specific and Practical

Human beings are creatures of habit, and the well-worn paths that our lives follow are habits we have developed throughout our lifetimes. Habits don't change overnight. Very few of us can just decide that we're going to change something and then sustain a new behavior without looking back. It takes time and patience to change longstanding habits. And it takes practice. Many manifestation teachings don't include specific practices to help embed the new habits of thought into the subconscious mind. In the chapters that follow, I'll help you create a personalized tool for transmitting your desires deep into your subconscious and out into the Universe, calibrating the vibrations to the perfect frequency for success.

3. Connecting to Purpose

The most important element for creating the life you want is to connect your individual dreams and desires to the greater good of the world in which you live. You are not creating your life in isolation. You are *cocreating* it with the Universe. Yes, you can have the life you want and fulfill all of your personal longings, but if it's all about you, ultimately you'll find that the power to deliver deep fulfillment will be limited. When we hear words like *manifestation*, *attraction*, and *creation*, we often associate them with getting. But the real power of the law of attraction is found when we shift our attention from *getting* to *giving*. Generosity, love, and service are not afterthoughts — things you think you'll have time, money, and energy for once you get what you want. The energy of compassion is what drives a truly cocreative engagement with the Universe. This book will teach you a method of manifestation that integrates the element of giving from the very beginning.

With these three essential keys in place, you truly can cocreate the life of your dreams. Are you ready to get to work? Because it will take work. If you're ready to experience lasting fulfillment in a world where the odds seem to be stacked against it, you'll need to dig deep to understand why your dreams seem to elude you. You'll need to study how the Universe works and learn how to make it work for you. You'll need to rethink your definition of happiness and root out the unhealthy vibrations of fear and subconscious cultural programming that may be blocking your creative energy. You'll need to become more sensitive to the vibrations of your own thoughts, feelings, and intentions and to those of the people in your sphere. And above all, you'll need to be committed, not just to your own happiness or success, but to the greater good of the world. Because if there's a "secret" that can change your life, it's this: We're all connected — from the smallest living being to the farthest star in the cosmos. Of course, that may be the oldest secret there is. But it remains a secret in that many of us live our entire lives without discovering its true transformative power. As you'll learn in this book, you can use this secret to manifest the life of your dreams, but it will also change what the life of your dreams means to you.

I've always been a straight shooter, and I won't promise you anything that I haven't tried and proven in my own life. I won't ask you to do anything I don't ask of myself. I won't tell you it will be easy — because it won't. I will tell you, however, that anything is possible. You truly can manifest the life you long for, and the tools in this book will help you do that.

Who Programmed Your Life?

So let's come back to the question the mystery man asked me: Why aren't you already living the life of your dreams? You may point to all kinds of reasons — your too-small salary and the mounting bills, the demands of other people, the kids still living at home, the divorce, your chronic health problems, your lack of a college degree, your poor career choices, and so on. And all of those reasons may be valid, to a point. But I've come to believe there's a deeper reason why so many of us live what Henry David Thoreau called "lives of quiet desperation."

Why do we feel unfulfilled and unhappy? Because we're running on someone else's program. Our habits — and the neural pathways that developed — were written by someone else. Subconsciously, we've all absorbed messages from the environment we grew up in and the culture that surrounds us, and these messages are running our lives, like the hidden programming that organizes your computer. That's one reason why, even when we think we want something else, we end up creating lives that perpetuate the same patterns we see all around us. And the essence of all the messages we receive — whether from parents, society, or the media — is the same: *fear.* "Life is not safe, and when something seems good, it's not to be trusted."

Understanding the Subconscious

The messages of fear and mistrust that we receive from our parents and our society embed themselves in our subconscious, or unconscious, minds. Psychologists, from Freud and Jung to more modern scholars, broadly agree that human beings form as many as 90 percent of their habits by the age of seven — in other words, these ways of acting and thinking become subconscious. Your subconscious has an amazing amount of processing power. While the conscious mind, according to neuroscientists, provides less than 5 percent of our cognitive activity during the day, the subconscious deals with the other 95 percent or more. Bruce Lipton says that the unconscious mind can process forty million nerve impulses per second, while the conscious mind only processes forty.[6] It's as if you have a giant supercomputer beneath the surface of your awareness!

Activities that have become subconscious are known as habits. Many of them are healthy, important habits. Indeed, our very lives depend on the fact that we learn to breathe and perform hundreds of other life-sustaining functions subconsciously. Neuroscientist David Eagleman calls these "zombie subroutines." He likens the conscious mind to the CEO of a company: "He sets the higher-level directions and assigns new tasks [but] he doesn't need to understand the software that each department in the organization uses.... As long as the zombie subroutines are running smoothly, the CEO can sleep."[7]

Here's another helpful analogy: The conscious mind is like a pilot flying a plane — his hand is on the wheel, and he's looking out for anything unusual, but most of the plane's functions run themselves. He doesn't have to think about keeping the engine running, the airspeed constant, or the altitude steady. And as a passenger, I'm glad I don't have to entrust my safety to one person's ability to hold all of that in consciousness. I'd rather have those things running on autopilot — although I'm glad the human pilot is there with all of his attention available to notice any anomalies.

It's the same when you're driving your car. You may not have an "autopilot" button, but many of your actions are automatic. Remember how, when you were learning to drive, you had to consciously remind yourself to check your mirrors, indicate, check your mirrors again, and so on? If you're a good driver, you now go through these routines without thinking about them.

As all these analogies show, the unconscious is a miraculous thing. What's also important to understand is that it can be problematic. It may contain beliefs or routines of thought and behavior that are toxic to your happiness — patterns of mental programming that prevent you from achieving your dreams, your desires, and your goals. This is a much bigger part of what drives you than you may realize.

To take the CEO metaphor a little further, imagine a company hiring a new leader, but the strategy and the culture that were shaped by the old leader remain very much in place. The new CEO is inspired and motivated to do things differently, but she immediately struggles against powerful currents. No matter how hard she tries, she can't get very far or make much progress until she deals with the strategy and the culture. This might mean making the old strategy conscious and then enrolling the team in a new one. It could involve shining a light on the company culture in various ways and shifting how people relate and work together.

I also like to think of the conscious mind as the top of an iceberg, or what's visible above the surface of the ocean. The subconscious mind is the enormous bulk beneath the waves. The subconscious mind is permeable to the influence of others, society, and the life circumstances we find ourselves in. It's not just a personal set of beliefs, habits, and ideas. In fact, C. G. Jung believed we have a "collective unconscious," which might explain some of the deeper currents that drive us — patterns and archetypes that seem to go beyond even the scope of our own life experiences. Imagine that the iceberg not only extends deep beneath the waves but connects to a vast subterranean ice continent.

This is a critical piece of information for anyone who wants to have a better life. Why? Because the number-one block to creating the life you want is the way you've been programmed by your family and by culture and society. Even if you grew up in a family that was relatively happy and free of trauma, you've probably absorbed a fear-based belief system from the culture around you — from your teachers, your friends, your friends' parents, and, of course, from the media. Even your most well-intentioned friends are probably unknowingly coaching you to be fearful and self-protective. And those programmed attitudes, thoughts, and beliefs send out particular vibrations into the Universe.

Here are some examples of common beliefs:
"I am born a sinner."
"I'm not good enough."
"No one loves me."
"I'm alone."
"I must do more to be worthy."
"I don't have enough."

The quality of your life is based on a cycle of thinking that starts deep in your subconscious. These thoughts create our reality. This cycle of thoughts becoming reality goes something like this:

A lousy belief about yourself or the world creates
    a lousy thought.
This lousy thought creates a lousy emotion.
The emotion gives rise to a less-than-ideal action.
That action creates an undesirable result.
A series of results, all springing from that funda-
    mentally lousy belief, create a life of limitation
    and suffering — a dismal destiny.

By asking you to take responsibility for creating all of this, you may think I'm being too harsh. That's how I felt when the mystery man told me I'd created my own suffering. Today, I run into so many people who want to play the victim card, perpetually living as if they are not responsible for their lives. Victimization is the real trap.

Take back your power! You have the power, no matter what the circumstance, to take responsibility. What is responsibility? It's your *ability* to *respond*. What are you going to do now? No matter how or why you ended up in a particular circumstance, you can take responsibility for your reaction to it. You can choose to be the victim or the victor.

Surface Thoughts versus Subconscious Programming

Now that you understand the role of the subconscious and the cycle of thought, perhaps it's clearer why simply "changing your thoughts," as so many people advise, is not enough to change your life. You can make as much effort as you want to think more positive thoughts but still not "attract" the things you long for. This is because the positive thinking is just happening on the surface; it is drowned out by the much more powerful vibrations of your subconscious programming.

For example, you may believe you want love and even spend time trying to attract your soul mate into your life. But if you've been subconsciously programmed to not trust other people and to never open up, you'll actually be energetically pushing away the possibility of connection. If you believe you're not worthy of love, you'll prove yourself right again and again.

Or you may declare that you want to be wealthy, and you work hard to earn a good living. But if you've been programmed to believe you're not truly valuable, you'll likely find yourself repelling the wealth and abundance you long for at an energetic level, since you are sending the Universe a message that you don't deserve it.

Here's another important truth: Your subconscious doesn't judge. It will deliver on whatever you believe, no matter whether it is true or not, and no matter whether it makes you happy or miserable.

One of the first books I read about manifestation after my encounter with the mystery man — and one that had a deep influence on me — was Joseph Murphy's *The Power of Your Subconscious Mind*. He explained that "if your blueprint is full of mental patterns of fear, worry, anxiety, or lack, and if you are despondent, doubtful, and cynical, then the texture of the mental material you are weaving into your mind will come forth as more toil, care, tension, anxiety, and limitation of all kinds."[8]

Author Gregg Braden, a powerful thinker on these matters, expands on this idea: "In the instant of our first breath, we are infused with the single greatest force in the universe — the power to translate the possibilities of our minds into the reality of our world. To fully awaken to our power, however, requires a subtle change in the way we think of ourselves in life, a shift in belief." He explains, "Just the way sound creates visible waves as it travels through a droplet of water, our 'belief waves' ripple through the quantum fabric of the universe to become our bodies and the healing, abundance, and peace — or disease, lack, and suffering — that we experience in life. And just the way we can tune a sound to change its patterns, we can tune our beliefs to preserve or destroy all that we cherish, including life itself." As we tune our beliefs and develop our power to consciously cocreate our reality, we are, as he puts it, "never more than a belief away from our greatest love, deepest healing, and most profound miracles."[9]

In line with this thinking, you have to change the subconscious patterns of your being — your blueprint, as Murphy called it, or your belief waves, in Braden's terms — to reflect abundance and fulfillment if you are going to attract abundance and fulfillment into your life. If your subconscious mind is convinced that you are wounded, deprived, and needy, that is what you will manifest. To quote one of the greatest contemporary manifestation teachers, the late Wayne Dyer: "For me, manifesting is not about attracting what you want. Manifesting is an awareness and an understanding that you attract what you are."[10]

Another of my favorite lines by Wayne Dyer is the title of one of his books: *You'll See It When You Believe It*. If you want to see your heart's desires manifest in your life, you first need to believe in them. To do that, you probably need to root out some unconscious beliefs that are getting in the way. You may not be able to immediately access the patterns or beliefs that are blocking you — because they're in your subconscious, which by definition is beyond the reach of your conscious mind. But if you look at the life you've manifested for yourself, you'll see the beliefs it reflects. Therefore, to cocreate a different life, you can't just rearrange the conscious thoughts at the surface of your mind — you need to find a way to access your subconscious and reprogram yourself at that level. You need to learn to write your own program and override the one that was written for you before you had a choice.

You have the ability to purge the negative beliefs and thoughts that lead to a lousy life. Through the application of disciplined action and effective tools, you can reprogram the negative thoughts of the subconscious mind. This process of forsaking negative programmed beliefs takes tenacity. You need to be willing to question everything you believe. Question everything I tell you as well! It takes effort and discernment to drill down and get to the truth.

The good news is that while your subconscious mind is permeable to the negative programming around you, it is also connected to the creative energy of the Universe. When you learn how to work with energy and vibrations, you can use your subconscious to tap into the field of divine abundance and love.

Here's the best news of all: The only way you can fail is to do nothing. So don't be afraid to start and have it not go spectacularly right away. Yes, I know you probably think you've tried and failed many times, setting your resolutions on January 1 and quitting the gym by February. But this is different. If you start, you can't fail! And you'll realize how easy and simple life can be if you just follow the simple steps I'll be teaching you. As the old saying goes, the journey of a hundred miles begins with a single step.

My Number-One Desire

My first step, as I sat in the mystery man's kitchen, was to identify my number-one desire. Well, that was easy. Nothing was more important to me, at that moment in my life, than being reconciled with my wife and baby daughter.

Taking out a blank sheet of paper and a pencil, the mystery man asked me to describe this dream. "Imagine you are an artist, and with your words, you are going to paint a wonderful picture that represents how you truly want your life to be." He specified that I must describe this vision not as a future hope but as if it were a current reality. "This is important," he explained, "because time is not real."

I decided to ignore that comment, since I had no idea what he was talking about. He immediately detected the skepticism behind my silence and turned to Einstein for backup: "The distinction between past, present, and future is only a stubbornly persistent illusion." Well, who was I to argue with Einstein?

The mystery man also told me that my description of my dream had to be emotionally powerful and authentic, in order to break the illusion in my subconscious mind that this was not currently true and to allow the energy that flows through the Universe, which he referred to as *God*, to make it an actual reality.

"There's a science to writing intentions," he told me. "When you return for your session next week, I'll explain the formula that we'll be using." I still wasn't sure that there would be a session next week, but I figured I might as well get my money's worth this time around, so I focused on writing out my number-one dream, following the instructions he'd given. Here is the statement we crafted:

> My wife, Lisa, and I are happily married. Every single day our love for one another grows deeper and stronger. I am so grateful to feel such great peace and love. My wife loves and adores me and I love and adore her. Our love empowers me to be a better version of myself. Our life and love is beautiful and inspires others. Our daughter, Michelle, thrives in this spirit of love. Both parents love her very much and she returns this love unconditionally. I feel so amazingly blessed. All three of us are so happy. I love my marriage and my life!

Writing this was not an easy task for me because my emotional state and the reality of my situation could not have been further from what the words described. Lisa hated me, rightfully so, and my daughter was growing up without a father in her life. It took about forty-five minutes to get the statement written to the mystery man's satisfaction.

"Now what?" I asked.

"That's all for today," he replied, repeating his assurance that in the seventh week of our work together, he would teach me a magical technique that would make it impossible for my written word not to become a reality. "Before we meet next week, think about what dream you would like to work on next."

I nodded, eager to get out of there. The hour I had spent with him hadn't made me feel better — in fact, I felt worse because he'd brought all my pain to the surface, like a raw wound exposed to the rain and biting wind. As I drove away from the session, my arm out the window holding the door shut, I couldn't help but wonder if I had just wasted $50. This was more than I would make in tips that night after taking eight hours of abuse from drunk diners. But despite myself, somehow I knew that next week I'd be back.

2

The Intention Creation Formula

WEEK TWO

If you limit your choices only to what seems possible or reasonable, ...you disconnect yourself from what you truly want, and all you have left is a compromise.

— Robert Fritz, *The Path of Least Resistance*

The following week, the sun was shining as I drove through the sleepy suburban neighborhoods to the mystery man's house.

He opened the door with a warm and sweet smile. "I had a feeling you would come back. You really do want to change your life. I promise you, I won't waste your time."

I handed him $50 in cash — the sum total of my tips for the week. Damn, I hated my job at the restaurant. It was badly run, the staff were treated poorly, the food sucked, and it was little wonder the customers didn't feel like being generous when they paid their bills. I wished

I could quit, but I desperately needed the money. My checking account was nearly overdrawn after paying my monthly child support. As I mulled over the sorry state of my financial affairs, my doubts rose again, clouding over the short-lived feeling of hope I'd had when I knocked on the door.

The mystery man seemed to sense my change of mood. "Don't focus on your fears," he told me. "Remember, thoughts are things. Whatever you give your attention to will send a vibration out into the Universe. Let's continue the adventure of creating the life you truly want and begin moving from where you are to where you want to be. What dream do you want to work on today?"

In that moment, I realized I'd forgotten to do my homework. Grasping for whatever was at the top of my mind, it occurred to me that the restaurant would be a much better place to work and to eat if I was in charge. So I blurted out, "I want to own my own business."

He smiled. "Well, let's get to work."

Desires, he explained, must be empowered by turning them into clear intentions. It is not enough to have a vague sense of direction — it needs to be brought fully into conscious awareness. "We instinctively move toward what we really want," he told me, "when we become consciously aware of what it is."

This time, as we worked on my statement, he taught me more about the particular style in which he was asking me to write my intentions. "These are not just words on paper," he insisted. "You need to create a vibrant, multi-sensory life vision of what you truly want."

In the years since, I've distilled his invaluable advice into an eight-point Intention Creation Formula. Following this formula, you can write your intentions in such clear and powerful language that when they are transmitted, the atoms of the Universe will rearrange themselves to create the life you truly desire. When implemented faithfully, this formula will energize your intentions and remove any subconscious thought barriers that might otherwise inhibit their manifestation. Each of the eight points described below is designed to amplify the vibrational frequency with which your intentions are broadcast into the Universe. This formula is central to activating the Creation Frequency.

The Intention Creation Formula

The Intention Creation Formula has eight parts, all of which need to be taken into account as you write your intentions:

1. Present Tense
2. Positive Language
3. Emotionally Powerful and Authentic
4. Spirit of Gratitude
5. What You Truly Desire
6. Eliminate Judgment

7. Infinite Possibility
8. Upgrade as You Evolve

Let's go through these one at a time.

1. Present Tense

Describe your intention not as a future hope or dream, but as if it were a current reality. Write as if the outcome of the intention is already in existence, as if the perfect scenario already exists. Visualize how you see your life and evoke the way it feels when your intention is fully manifest. Write from the outcome.

To the mind and the trillions of cells in the body, there is no difference between reality and imagination. Time is nonlinear. We are in the ever-present now. The Universe works in the present moment, not in an imagined future. You are proclaiming what is now. This is faith. You know it before you see it. When you know it, then you see it.

2. Positive Language

The Universe does not understand negative language — words like *not* or terms expressing lack. Writing in positive language means writing about what you *do* want, not about what you *don't* want. When I told the mystery man I wanted to write, "I am no longer in debt," he explained that including the word *debt* communicates the vibration of lack, even though it was prefaced by "no longer." It is better to write, "I have an abundance of money."

Similarly, if you write the intention "My wife and I no longer fight," the Universe only hears the word *fight*, and you might get more conflict, not less. The same sentiment expressed in positive language might read: "My wife and I have a loving and peaceful relationship." Or, if your intention is to find a job that is no longer boring and tedious, write, "I have a fulfilling and impactful career." State what you desire rather than avoiding what is unpleasant.

3. Emotionally Powerful and Authentic

Use feeling words that activate your heart and elicit an emotional response. Emotion is energy in motion. Emotion puts your intention into motion. Your emotions each carry a particular vibrational frequency out into the Universe. When you infuse your intentions with high-frequency emotions like enthusiasm, joy, gratitude, generosity, and love, they will resonate more powerfully — an important idea that I'll return to in the next chapter. Ideally, every one of your intentions should include the emotion of love.

When you attach high-frequency emotions to your intentions, you supercharge them. This is another reason why it's important not to use negative language, since the emotional frequencies of those terms tend to be low, and they may sabotage your creative process.

It's not enough to just add emotional words to your statement. You need to envision yourself actually achieving your goals and, most importantly, to feel the emotions that this gives rise to.

In fact, if you're struggling to get clear about your intentions, you may want to take a tip from Danielle LaPorte, author of *The Desire Map*, and start with the emotions you want to feel. She points out that, when you set goals, "You're not chasing the goal itself — you're chasing the feelings that you hope attaining those goals will give you." When we don't realize this, she explains, "We have the procedures of achievement upside down. Typically we come up with our to-do lists, our bucket lists, and our strategic plans — all the stuff we want to have, get, accomplish, and experience outside of ourselves."[1] Then we desperately hope that we'll feel fulfilled when we get there. Danielle's suggestion is to first get clear on how you want to feel in your life and then create intentions for getting there. She challenges us to let our most desired feelings consciously inform how we plan our days, our careers, and our lives. Give it a try!

Another reason why it's important to really feel the emotions is that the subconscious mind does not know the difference between imagination and reality. We all know how this works with things we're afraid of. If we dwell on our fear, we can convince ourselves that our fear is real, and too often we will actually set in motion the very events we're trying to avoid. Your subconscious becomes fully convinced of the reality of your worst nightmares, as does your body, sometimes moving into full-out fight-or-flight mode. In the same way, if you can make an imagined goal emotionally convincing, your subconscious mind won't know the difference. In doing this, you open the door within your subconscious for the needed energy to flow out into the Universe to make it reality.

4. Spirit of Gratitude

Write from a place of gratitude — the kind of gratitude you would feel if you had already received your desire. Gratitude is associated with positive emotions, hence it will automatically raise your frequency. Expressing gratitude opens the heart, connecting you to the energy of love and abundance and readying you to receive. It is very easy to deliver what is desired into an open heart. Be a receiver.

5. What You Truly Desire

An essential element of becoming a successful creator is knowing what you *really* want. Your desires are an expression of the uniqueness of your soul. Your intentions should be what you truly desire — not what your parents, spouse, or friends think your life should look like. We are all programmed with beliefs of what life should look like. Throw those out and write your desires as if you were a playful child, not letting the "cares of the world" dictate your fullest expression. Be empowered to get what you really want.

Desire is powerful. As the Buddhist teacher Mark

Epstein writes, "Desire is a teacher: When we immerse ourselves in it without guilt, shame, or clinging, it can show us something special about our own minds that allows us to embrace life fully."[2]

This is not something we tend to devote enough energy to doing. Most people spend more time planning their vacations than they do planning how they truly want to spend their lives. We may start out with grand ambitions and plans, but culture has programmed us to expect less and less as we get older and to be afraid of failure. Too often, people quit dreaming sometime in their twenties. This is tragic. Too many people "die with all their music in them," as Oliver Wendell Holmes Sr. wrote. Invest the time to connect deeply with yourself and find out what you *really* want.

The answer to the question "What do I really want?" may change at different times in your life, but the key is to answer it as fully and as authentically as you can for this moment, right now. No one else can define what your life's desires are, so you must be willing to question yourself rigorously and deeply.

6. Eliminate Judgment

Honor your heart's true desire and trust that it is for the highest good of all involved. Do not judge anything your heart reveals as its aim. Allow your heart to play fully and be totally fulfilled. There is no ranking system for how worthy your intention is. It is not like spiritual intentions get fifty points and material intentions get only ten. Life is a holistic process. All intentions are part of the same perfect wholeness that you are.

7. Infinite Possibility

Write intentions from a space of infinite possibility. Don't squish your intentions down to fit the size of your current consciousness. Write intentions in a way that will cause your consciousness to grow in the fulfillment of them. Recognize your limiting beliefs and don't let them influence how you write your intentions.

We humans are programmed to constantly second-guess ourselves and life. We are afraid to fail, and so we imagine every possible scenario that might trip us up. In the process, we often talk ourselves out of the things we really want. My friend Marcia Wieder, who is also my personal "dream coach," says, "The number-one way we sabotage our dreams is by projecting fear and doubt into them." She advises people to acknowledge the fear and doubt that they are feeling in the present moment, "but don't let it into your dreams. Otherwise, when you move toward your dreams you'll be moving toward your doubts."[3]

Doubts and limitations usually begin with a "but," and they are often related to not having enough money, time, energy, and so on. In removing limitations, I find it helpful to ask myself, "What would I do if money were not an object?" and "What would I do if I knew I could not fail?" Tell yourself that the Universe will provide abundant resources for whatever you desire to create, and then take a fresh look at your dreams and intentions.

That said, you may want to add in a dash of realism, too. As I write these words, I am sixty years old. I am not going to be a running back in the NFL, no matter how powerful my intention. However, my intention might be filled in another way, like being a football coach with a running back as my star protégé. Removing limitations from your dreams doesn't mean you're going to ignore real constraints. But make sure the intentions you create are free of the vibrations of fear and doubt.

The bottom line, when writing your intentions, is this: Just use your heart. Don't let your head tell you what is and what is not possible. The Universe is far more powerful than the limited conditioning of your thinking.

8. Upgrade as You Evolve

When writing your intentions, be specific (your intentions will be more powerful if they are concrete and detailed), but don't be attached to the details. The Universe might surprise you by delivering something that looks quite different than you imagined it would be. You may also adapt and improve your intentions as time passes — they are not written in stone. They are written in energy, and energy is very malleable.

A common reason people get stuck when writing their intentions is that they treat their intentions as if they will never be able to change them. This becomes a reason to never move on to the next necessary steps in manifesting the life you dream of. Here's my advice: *Relax!* You can change your intentions anytime you want. In fact, because life is constantly changing and you are, too, I would expect your intentions to evolve and develop as you and your circumstances shift. For now, all you have to do is write the most authentic and emotionally powerful expression of what you want *right now*.

If what you want changes tomorrow, you can revise or rewrite your intention.

If you gain a new insight, you can upgrade your statement. Allow your intention to be a process that guides your evolution. Some intentions may serve you through your lifetime, some may need to be adapted as you evolve, and some that manifest will be replaced by new ones. Intentions are a conversation with the Universe, an ever-expanding dialogue. They are dynamic. Let them flow.

Expressing Your Heart's Desires

You can see each of the elements of the Intention Creation Formula reflected in the statement I crafted during that second session with the mystery man:

> I own my own business, and I love it. I focus on taking care of my customers and employees. I love my customers and employees, and in return, they love me. My wife and daughter support me in our business. It makes me feel incredibly happy that they can be there with me. Our family is so

supported by our business and by the love we receive from our employees and customers. My business grows stronger every day, and I am so very grateful. People from all over the area hear about our business and how special it is; it becomes the talk of the town. I am deeply grateful to be able to do what I love. I experience joy each day that fills me with the energy to work harder and serve more customers.

Note the number of powerful, positive emotions contained in this simple paragraph — love, joy, care, and gratitude. As I read it now, I can feel the power vibrating through those emotions, just as I did when I sat at the mystery man's table and read the finished statement aloud for the first time.

I can also still remember how hard this was to write. It was difficult to convincingly express something that felt so far-fetched. Sometimes when writing our intentions, we hold back on the emotional level out of fear or doubt that they might really come true. Especially if you've tried and failed before, you may be hesitant to shoot too high. All of your fears and doubts may rise to the surface, trying to convince you that what you want is not possible. For me, what came up as I tried to write was the fact that I'd never finished school, let alone gotten a college degree. I had no management experience and no capital. Being a wealthy business owner seemed close to impossible in my near future, but deep down I knew it was what I wanted. I hated the way my boss treated me and the other employees at the restaurant, and even with my limited experience, I could see that he was running the business into the ground. I wanted to prove that it could be done better.

What are your dreams? Can you come up with a list of your heart's desires? To begin, just brainstorm freely. It doesn't matter how many desires you write down — later, I'll share some advice on how to prioritize.

Pick one and follow the Intention Creation Formula. You may find the process challenging, but without going through this challenge to the other side, you'll never be able to manifest your desires and truly ease your pain. Take the most important of your intentions and write a paragraph in the present tense. Ensure that it is emotionally powerful, authentic, and phrased in positive terms, using the previous examples as models. Here are some questions to help guide you as you write:

What does my life look like when I have fulfilled my intention?

What emotions arise when I imagine having attained this goal?

Where do I visualize myself being when this dream becomes a reality? Am I in a specific place that I can describe?

> How does my achievement affect those around
> me? What do they do or say?

As you answer these questions, I hope your intention starts to take shape. As you work on it, take the time to search for words and expressions that are authentic to you. Your subconscious is sensitive, and it will not be convinced by something half-hearted or inauthentic. Can you feel your statement's vibration when you read it aloud? Does it jump off the page? Do you feel excited, inspired, and uplifted when you read it? Do you feel the resonance of love, joy, gratitude, or generosity? Don't worry if there are voices in your head telling you that what you've written down is impossible, unrealistic, or pie-in-the-sky. If the words you have written light you up, then stay focused on that uplifting feeling. The steps I'll guide you through next will take care of your fears and prove your doubts wrong.

As you are reading the next few chapters, set aside some time to work on writing out each of your intentions, using the Intention Creation Formula. In chapter 7, you'll learn the secret to making them a reality.

3

How the Universe Really Works

WEEK THREE

If you want to find the secrets of the universe,
think in terms of energy, frequency, and vibration.
— Nikola Tesla

The next week, I'd done my homework. As I pulled up at
the mystery man's house for my third session, I knew the
intention I wanted to work on. I wanted to earn $10,000 a
month. Back then, this was an unthinkable sum of money
for me. I made less than a quarter of that, working two
jobs, and I had no qualifications to my name. How in the
world was I supposed to bring in that kind of money?

My mentor had told me to set my sights high, however,
so I firmly banished all doubts as I knocked on his door.

"Well, someone has a different vibration today," the
mystery man declared, the moment he set eyes on me.
Once again, I was amazed at how he seemed to know what
I was feeling and thinking before I'd even said a word.

"Are you psychic or something?" I asked, as I took my now-familiar seat at his kitchen table.

"It's really not that mysterious," he replied. "I'm just tuned in."

Tuning In to the Vibrational Field

It would be many years before I truly understood the meaning of the mystery man's cryptic statement. He never explained the science of frequency — how could he, when much of it was not even available at that time? However, I have no doubt that in some mysterious way he intuited things that some of the brightest minds in science illuminated only later. He truly was "tuned in" — perhaps more so than anyone else I've met.

Have you ever sat in a great concert hall and listened to the cacophony of an orchestra tuning up? The jarring clash of notes, the harsh scraping of bows on strings, the mess of uncoordinated sound. While the audience gets settled in, each musician leans over his or her instrument, listening intently and carefully while adjusting the pitch, seemingly oblivious to the surrounding chaos. After a few minutes, they fall silent, but the air is left humming. Then the house lights go down, the conductor lifts the baton, and the discord is washed away by the perfect harmony that floods the auditorium.

When you are going about your day-to-day business, even right now as you're reading this book, you're actually in the midst of something very similar to that tuning-up period before the concert begins. As chemistry professor Donald Hatch Andrews wrote, "The universe is more like music than like matter."[1] Music is made up of vibrations calibrated to certain frequencies, which become sound. And everything in the Universe — from Earth itself to the natural world to the objects around you — is made up of energy and vibrations. Your very own thoughts and feelings are also vibrating, carrying their unique energetic currents out into the Universe. Are they resonating in harmony with the world around you, creating a life of beautiful music? Or are they discordant and out of tune? In order to cocreate the life you want, you need to learn how to *tune in* to the vibrations of your own thoughts and feelings, of the people around you, and of the world we live in, and then *tune up* your personal vibrations to bring about a more harmonious life. In order to do that, you need to understand some basic facts about how the Universe works.

Four Life-Changing Truths about the Universe

I'm not a physicist; I'm a businessman. But I'm also someone who cares deeply about helping people live happier, healthier, more harmonious lives. For that reason, I've become quite passionately interested in physics and, in particular, the relatively new science of quantum physics. Quantum physics offers us a window into how the Universe works, at its most elementary, microscopic level. However abstract and esoteric that might sound, it is actually profoundly relevant to you and me and our everyday lives. By understanding the nature of reality, you can change *your* reality.

Over the past forty or fifty years, countless popular books, as well as several films, have gone into great depth explaining the basic principles of this complex science and interpreting what these principles could mean about life, consciousness, God, and you and me. Sometimes these efforts blur the line between science and speculation, but they also make courageous attempts to go where science cannot go and to connect the dots between things like physics and mysticism, quantum reality and human intention.

I'd like to share with you four of the basic concepts I've learned, in the simplest terms I can, drawing on the work of some of my favorite writers who have helped to translate these ideas for those of us without a degree in physics. I hope you will forgive any oversimplifications. My intention is simply to offer a brief overview of some of the ideas that have been most meaningful to me and that are integral to the way I approach the business of creating the life you long for. If you find these ideas as fascinating as I do, I would encourage you to pursue that interest beyond what I share in these pages. Study, research, educate yourself, and live the life of your dreams! You might begin by digging deeper into some of the books I mention, or searching YouTube or Google. You may find these new ideas disconcerting, but that could be a good sign — after all, as the Danish physicist Niels Bohr wrote, "Anyone who is not shocked by quantum theory has not understood it."[2] Then again, American physicist Richard Feynman declared, "I think I can safely say that nobody understands quantum mechanics."[3] So if you find this stuff confusing, you're certainly not alone. I'd encourage you to simply open your mind to these ideas and let them dislodge your familiar views on reality a little. As we move into this book, you'll have the opportunity to test them out for yourself and see if they make sense to you.

1. Matter Is an Illusion

Here's the most important scientific fact I've ever learned about the Universe: Everything is energy. That may sound like something you'd hear from a spiritual teacher rather than a scientist — and indeed, wise men and women have been saying such things for millennia — but these days, it is in fact a widely accepted scientific truth. Einstein declared that "mass and energy are both but different manifestations of the same thing."[4] Max Planck, a Nobel Prize–winning German physicist and a contemporary of Einstein, who many consider to be the father of quantum theory, wrote the following:

> As a man who has devoted his whole life to the most clear headed science, to the study of matter, I can tell you as a result of my research about atoms this much: There is no matter as such. All matter originates and exists only by virtue of a

force which brings the particles of an atom to vibration and holds this most minute solar system of the atom together.[5]

Since Planck's groundbreaking statement, the growing field of quantum physics has continued to shed light on this truth and its profound implications. It has shown us that physical atoms, once considered the "building blocks" of matter, are actually like vortices of energy — spinning and vibrating. Do you remember learning about atoms in chemistry class? Each atom is a nucleus with electrons rotating around it, and the quantity and shape of the electrons and their orbits result in the particular set of vibrational frequencies. One of the most amazing things about atoms that I didn't learn in school is that they are 99 percent empty space!

The smallest identifiable units of energy are known as *quanta*. But they are not really "things." Here's where it gets very strange indeed: They are both visible particles and invisible waves, and they fluctuate between these two states. As journalist and author Lynne McTaggart puts it, "What we believe to be our stable, static universe is in fact a seething maelstrom of subatomic particles fleetingly popping in and out of existence."[6] However improbable it may seem as we walk through our lives on the solid Earth, matter is an illusion. The Universe is more like a dance of energy, a shifting pattern of vibrations.

What I love about this discovery is that it validates what mystics have been saying for hundreds if not thousands of years. The ancient Hindu text Rig Veda says in its creation hymn, "There was neither nonexistence nor existence then."[7] The Buddhist scriptures point to the impermanence of form. The Sufi mystical poet Rumi described how to his awakened eyes, "Every tree and plant in the meadow seemed to be dancing, those which average eyes would see as fixed and still."

I had my own mystical vision roughly fifteen years ago. It didn't happen in a church or sacred place, nor in some beautiful natural setting — I was just lying on my bed one Saturday afternoon, and my wife was lying beside me. I was holding her close, so our energies were physically connected. We may have been listening to music or talking, but we had fallen silent, and a kind of meditative state descended on the room. I could hear her breathing, so I started to sync my breathing to hers, and all of a sudden, my consciousness altered radically. My physical body and hers dissolved along with the bed, the room, and everything around it. All that remained was a sea of pure energy — millions of atoms vibrating.

After about ten minutes, the experience faded, but the memory of it has never left me. It was as if, for those few minutes, I was given a glimpse behind the illusion of matter and physical form, and I was allowed to directly see and feel the nature of reality. I had never experienced anything close to it before that moment, although it's happened several times since. What I have come away with each time is a deep conviction that who we are, at our most essential level, is not separate from the energy of the Universe, and the quality of that energy is love.

That's all very well for me to say. But interestingly, even some scientists speak about their discoveries in similarly mystical terms. In the 1970s, the physicist Fritjof Capra published his classic book *The Tao of Physics*, in which he speculates that perhaps "physics leads us today to a world view which is essentially mystical."[8] In the book's preface, he describes a powerful experience where all the things he *knew* theoretically as a physicist became directly apparent to him:

> Being a physicist, I knew that the sand, rocks, water, and air around me were made of vibrating molecules and atoms, and that these consisted of particles which interacted with one another by creating and destroying other particles. I knew also that the Earth's atmosphere was continually bombarded by showers of "cosmic rays," particles of high energy undergoing multiple collisions as they penetrated the air.... But until that moment I had only experienced it through graphs, diagrams, and mathematical theories. As I sat on that beach...I "saw" cascades of energy coming down from outer space, in which particles were created and destroyed in rhythmic pulses; I "saw" the atoms of the elements and those of my body participating in this cosmic dance of energy; I felt its rhythm and I "heard" its sound, and at that

moment I *knew* that this was the Dance of Shiva,
the Lord of Dancers worshipped by the Hindus.[9]

Have you ever had a moment like that, when you
seemed to see beyond or beneath the surface of the physical world? If so, think back to those moments in your
life and see if you can remember the sense of vibration.
If you've never had that experience, don't worry. You
may not be able to see, feel, and hear the cosmic dance of
atoms that surrounds you right now, but it is something
you can learn to tune in to. Whether you consider yourself a scientist, a mystic, or just a regular person like me,
you can become more sensitive to the vibrations of the
Universe. And in so doing, you can learn to play your
part in that dance in a more creative, intentional way.

2. Anything Is Possible

The discovery that everything is energy, not matter,
has some exciting implications. What quantum physicists have revealed to us is that while we tend to think of
atoms as looking like little solar systems, they are actually
more like clouds or fields of possibility. Remember, they
are 99 percent empty space! German theoretical physicist Werner Heisenberg explained that "the atoms or elementary particles themselves are not as real: they form
a world of potentialities and possibilities rather than one
of things and facts."[10] In other words, they exist in a kind
of suspended state, their identities still fluid and undeter-
mined. McTaggart describes each subatomic particle as

"a potential of any one of its future selves — or what is known by physicists as a 'superposition,' or sum, of all probabilities." Matter, at its most elemental, she writes, "isn't *anything* yet. Subatomic reality resembled...an ephemeral prospect of seemingly infinite options." For those of us who might find that a little too vague or esoteric, she compares it to "unset Jell-O."[11]

If everything in this Universe is made up of pure potential, then so are you! After all, these strange quantum nonobjects are the building blocks of reality, coming into form as the world you live in and your very own body. And just as the atoms that make up your body are not fixed, predictable objects, neither are the circumstances of your life. You are full of infinite possibility in every moment. It's your nature!

3. Consciousness Turns Possibility into Reality

If all of this wasn't disconcerting enough, quantum physics has discovered something even more bizarre. The presence of human consciousness seems to play an important role in determining which "future self" a quantum particle becomes. It exists in its state of infinite possibility until it is observed or measured by the instruments of science, and then it "collapses" into a particular entity. In other words, when you become aware of it, the Jell-O sets.

Attempting to explain this "observer effect," as it's known, has led some scientists to the conclusion that human consciousness is not simply a witness to the world, but may in fact play a "participatory" role in the creative dance of subatomic reality. Could human consciousness be in some way responsible for forcing particles out of a "probable" state and into a set state? As strange as it sounds, that's what a large number of very smart people believe. "This astounding observation also had shattering implications about the nature of reality," writes McTaggart. "It suggested that the consciousness of the observer brought the observed object into being. Nothing in the universe existed as an actual 'thing' independently of our perception of it. Every minute of every day we were creating our world."[12]

This may be a bit of a stretch for the imagination. Does it mean that the world doesn't exist if we're not looking? Physicists and their many interpreters have argued about this at great length. But whatever conclusion you draw, the data clearly indicates that human consciousness plays a participatory role in determining reality — something that you can learn to use to your advantage.

4. Everything Is Connected

Modern science is now increasingly able to demonstrate what mystics have always intuited — that everything is actually connected. The Universe is not a collection of separate objects but is a web of interconnected energetic processes. One of the most powerful demonstrations of this in the field of quantum physics is the "twin" photon experiment performed in 1997 by Dr. Nicolas Gisin and his colleagues at the University of Geneva. Gisin sent pairs of photons in opposite directions, to villages north and south of Geneva, along optical fibers like those used to transmit telephone calls. Reaching the ends of these fibers, the photons were forced to make random choices between alternative, equally possible pathways. The results showed that the paired photons always made the same decisions, even though no explanation could be found in the laws of classical physics that would allow for such "nonlocal" coordination or communication. This phenomenon is sometimes known as "quantum entanglement," and I believe it is clear evidence of the deeper, underlying interconnectedness of all of life.

Many people have speculated about the nature of the invisible but identifiable connections between the most basic particles of reality. McTaggart calls this connectedness "the Field," explaining, "Human beings and all living things are a coalescence of energy in a field of energy connected to every other thing in the world. This pulsating energy field is the central engine of our being and our consciousness."[13] Planck theorized that the Universe was held together by "a conscious and intelligent Mind [which] is the matrix of all matter."[14] The scientist David Bohm, who became friends with Einstein, also posited an invisible connecting structure that he called the "implicate order" or "enfolded order." Some people like to use more religious or spiritual terms to describe the same thing — *God*, *Source*, or *consciousness*.

Regardless of what we call the web of connections, the fact remains that *something* seems to be connecting everything — human beings, animals, plants, rocks, even the farthest stars. It could be said to be one of the few common principles taught by all the mystical and religious traditions: We are all one. We are all connected. As the contemporary spiritual teacher Eckhart Tolle writes, "Underneath your outer form, you are connected with something so vast, so immeasurable and sacred, that it cannot be conceived or spoken of — yet I am speaking of it now. I am speaking of it not to give you something to believe in but to show you how you can know it yourself."[15]

The reason it is so important to get in touch with the deeper, interconnected realm of consciousness is that it is your portal to the energy, intention, and creative potential of the Universe. Deepak Chopra, in *The Seven Spiritual Laws of Success*, writes, "The source of all creation is pure consciousness...pure potentiality seeking expression from the unmanifest to the manifest. And when we realize that our true Self is one of pure potentiality, we align with the power that manifests everything in the universe."[16]

If you are trying to cocreate from a shallower, more superficial sense of who you are, from a belief that you are only a separate individual, you will not be connected to the power of the Universe's intention. You will not be tapped into that source of power and drive that vibrates through everything around you. When you connect with your deeper self, and through that connect with the universal energy of consciousness, you will be directly tuning in to the Creation Frequency.

The Vibrations All Around You

So now that we've taken this brief — and hopefully not too bemusing — journey into the nature of reality, let's come back to you. As Penney Peirce writes in her book *Frequency*, "I want you to feel and imagine yourself as a porous, vibrational being merged into a vast field of vibrations; we are not solid lumps on a rock of a planet, but a collection of energies penetrating and being penetrated by millions of other energies."[17]

As you sit there right now, you are not solid, and neither is the chair you are sitting on, nor the book in your hands. These seemingly unyielding objects are dancing out of the field of possibility and coalescing in the light of your awareness. And you are connected to everyone and everything around you. You may not be able to see those connections, but I want to help you learn how to tune in to their vibrations and be able to interact with them more intentionally.

At every moment, you're surrounded by vibrational fields. Imagine yourself moving in a web of invisible currents of information. If you're reading from a tablet or e-reader, electromagnetic fields are emanating from that device — that's a fairly easy example to accept. But even if you're old-fashioned and you're holding a book made from paper, can you consider that it's not as solid as it appears? Because, as we just discussed, it is made up of energy, not matter. It is vibrating, even if you can't feel it.

If you don't believe in things you can't see, just tell me, how does that device in your pocket work? It's downloading vast quantities of information out of thin air!

You may not be able to hear these vibrations the way you hear the vibration of a violin string, but that is simply because their frequency is outside the range of ordinary human senses. *Frequency* simply means the speed at which something vibrates. The range of frequencies generates the spectrum of sound that we call the musical scale, but the frequencies don't stop there. The human ear is generally capable of hearing frequencies from approximately 15 Hz to 20,000 Hz (Hz, or hertz, measures the number of cycles of the repetitive wave form per second). But outside that range, all kinds of frequencies are not detectable by the human ear. I'm sure you know that dogs hear sounds we cannot hear, but that's just the beginning. There are higher and lower frequencies that are undetectable to the ordinary physical senses but that you can learn to tune in to with your subtler sensory capacities.

Let's start with some of the vibrations you can easily identify. If there are people around you, you can hear their voices. You may think they are speaking words, but actually their vocal chords are moving air molecules in a certain way that brings about a particular vibrational frequency, which gets picked up by your eardrum and digitized by your brain into zeros and ones. So language, like matter, is really an illusion! As you listen, you may hear words, but you can also tune in to the different vi-brations in tone. In a public place, like a coffee shop, it can be fun to pay attention just to the sounds people are making, rather than the words. The highly stressed mother trying to get her toddler to behave is clearly put-ting out an energy frequency different from the old man talking quietly to his wife as they sit in the sunshine. The group of young boys shouting to one another as they play soccer in the street is transmitting something dif-ferent from the teenage girls giggling as they pore over a magazine. The young couple whispering to each other over a shared chocolate muffin has an energy that is quite distinct from the two businessmen discussing a contract over coffee.

If you pay attention, you can hear the vibrations of voices. But what about the vibrations that you can't hear? You may be sensing these, even though you don't realize it. Why is it that you feel drawn to some people, but repelled by others? Why are some people calming and soothing in their presence, while others make us anxious or agitated? At some level, we're al-ways picking up on people's energy, and what that actu-ally means is that we're feeling their vibrations. As the hit song by the Beach Boys goes, "I'm picking up good vibrations."

When you pick up on the vibrations of others in the coffee shop, you're not just taking in their words or the tones of their voices. Their thoughts and emotions are also transmitting particular frequencies. The young mother may be depressed and desperate, and those feelings are vibrating heavily with the weight of her sadness. And she will attract more sadness toward herself if she continues to transmit those feelings to the Universe. One of the giggling girls may be deeply insecure and telling herself that she doesn't really fit in — that she's not thin enough or pretty enough. The young couple is buoyed up by new love, oblivious to anything around them. The businessmen are mistrustful and competitive, each convinced that the other is trying to take advantage. All of these emotions and thoughts are not just contained inside people's heads — they are being transmitted as vibrations into the field between them. Even other people's physical states give off vibrations — pain or tiredness or energy or pleasure.

Today we can measure the vibrational frequencies of matter. The Earth, for example, vibrates at 7.83 Hz on the scale of Schumann resonances, which is named after physicist Winfried Otto Schumann, who predicted it using mathematics back in 1952. Turns out the ancients were right when they talked about the "music of the spheres"!

Penney Peirce postulates that each of the energy frequencies of matter have matching consciousness frequencies. She correlates different brain wave frequencies with different states of consciousness, and she has developed a scale that maps the vibrations of everyday reality — your body, senses, thoughts, and emotions.

THE SCALES OF EVERYDAY VIBRATIONS

	BODY	SENSES	EMOTIONS	THOUGHTS
HIGH FREQUENCY fast/ expansive/ soul/love	Full presence	Communion	Love/ Empathy	Wisdom/ Oneness
	Perfect health	Direct experience	Generosity	Direct Knowing
	Joyful movement	Ultra-sensitivity	Joy/ Gratitude	Inspiration/ Insight
	Flexibility	Intuition	Enthusiasm	Fluid creativity
	Responsive-ness	Clairvoyance	Desire/ Motivation	Discovery/ Exploration
	Comfort/Rest	Clairaudience	Pleasure	Receptivity/ Openness
	Exhaustion	Clairsentience	Sincerity	Boredom/ Impatience
LOW FREQUENCY slow/dense ego/fear	Tension/ Stress	Vision	Contentment/ Trust	Distraction/ Absence
	Periodic pain	Hearing	Disappoint-ment	Projection/ Blame
	Chronic pain	Touch	Frustration	Logic/Proof
	Addiction	Taste	Doubt/ Insecurity	Beliefs/ Control games
	Disease/ Illness	Smell	Fear/Panic	Obsession
	Trauma/ Injury	Attraction/ Repulsion	Hate/Rage/ Refusal	Overwhelm
	Loss of function	Gut instinct	Guilt/Shame	Psychosis/ Neurosis
	Paralysis/ Coma	Subconscious Reaction	Depression/ Apathy	Suicidal

Copyright © 2009 by Penney Peirce. Reprinted by permission of the author.

Photographing Vibrations

If that sounds too "woo-woo," here's some amazing visual evidence: The Japanese researcher Masaru Emoto was able to photograph the effects of different vibrations on water crystals. First he experimented with music and found that the crystals formed different patterns depending on the music he played. Then he experimented with subtler vibrations — those associated with different words that relate to emotions. In his book *The Hidden Messages in Water*, he shares the results:

> It didn't seem logical for water to "read" the writing, understand the meaning, and change its form accordingly. But I knew from the experiment with music that strange things could happen. We felt as if we were explorers setting out on a journey through an unmapped jungle. The results of the experiments didn't disappoint us. Water exposed to "Thank you" formed beautiful hexagonal crystals, but water exposed to the word "Fool" produced crystals similar to the water exposed to heavy-metal music, malformed and fragmented.[18]

Reflecting on his experiments, he concludes, "Existence is vibration. The entire universe is in a state of vibration, and each thing generates its own frequency, which is unique.... My years of research into water have taught me that this is the fundamental principle of the universe." He adds, "The written words themselves actually emit a unique vibration that the water is capable of sensing. Water faithfully mirrors all the vibrations generated in the world, and changes these vibrations into a form that can be seen with the human eye. When water is shown a written word, it receives it as vibration, and expresses the message in a specific form."[19]

If you're wondering what invisible water crystals have to do with you and your life, remember, you are made up of 60 to 65 percent water!

Another person who has visually demonstrated the power of vibration is the YouTube artist Brusspup. I highly recommend you watch his videos to see for yourself. He attaches a black metal plate to a speaker and then pours sand onto it. As he plays different tonal frequencies through the speaker, the sand vibrates into intricate geometric patterns. The patterns become more complex as the frequency increases in pitch.

In the same way that the words Emoto wrote down were transmitting vibrations to the water, or that the music played on the speaker was transmitting its vibrations to the sand, your own thoughts and feelings are being transmitted out into the field of our interconnected Universe. Are they resonating harmoniously with the Universe, creating beautiful patterns, or are they out of tune, creating chaotic and fragmented imprints?

If you can learn to become more *attuned to* and *in tune with* the world around you, your life will change dramatically, I can assure you. In the collective field of vibrations, you can learn to engage in an energetic conversation and dialogue with other people and with the Universe. Through those conversations, you can harness the creative power to manifest the life you've always wanted.

You Are a Transmitter and a Receiver

"You have within you a *mighty power*, anxious and willing to serve you, a *power capable* of giving you *that which you earnestly desire*," wrote the early twentieth-century thinker R. H. Jarrett in his "little red book" *It Works*, a sixteen-page pamphlet that has been in print for more than a century. "To get what you want is no more mysterious or uncertain than the radio waves all around you. Tune in correctly and you get a perfect result, but to do this, it is, of course, necessary to know something of your equipment and have a plan of operation."[20]

So, what is your equipment? Essentially, your entire body is a tool through which you receive and transmit information. Your body is in constant relationship with the Universe — downloading information from the quantum field and uploading information into the quantum field. There are three major players in this universal dance of life: your DNA, your brain, and your heart.

First, let's talk about DNA. DNA receives every pulse from the Universe and transmits back into the Universe our unique frequency — messages about who we are and what we want. Our DNA represents our entire genetic blueprint. Dr. Fritz-Albert Popp proved that light emissions are emanating from our DNA, the core reactor from which we are broadcasting our personal energy signature.

Dr. Bruce Lipton's work is proving that we can actually reprogram our DNA. What he has discovered is that the nucleus of a cell is not read only. It is actually read and write. Basically, the cell is a programmable device, in response to environmental information. Therefore, if you are dissatisfied with your blueprint, you can change it and broadcast a new message about yourself to the Universe.

Scientists have recently shown that emotion affects DNA. A group of researchers in the UK were studying depression and noticed unexpected metabolic changes in their cells that appeared to be a result of the depression.[21] And if a low-frequency emotion like depression has such an impact, imagine what impact a high-frequency emotion like love or gratitude must have. Researchers at the HeartMath Institute experimented with this by placing DNA in vials and then generating certain emotions as they held the vials. What they found was that the DNA altered its shape in response to different feelings! Love, gratitude, and appreciation caused the DNA to relax and the strands to unwind, while anger, frustration, and stress caused it to tighten up and even switch off many of its codes! When the positive feelings came back, these effects were reversed.[22]

Each one of our cells has forty-six human chromosomes (twenty-three pairs), which contain as many as three billion base pairs of DNA. Each of these billions of strands stores our personal information. If we can reorganize our beliefs, thoughts, feelings, and the vibrations we are transmitting at a cellular level, we can reprogram our own personal blueprint to attain any goal we desire.

Next, let's talk about the amazing lump of gray matter inside your skull: your brain. While there is much we still do not understand about this complex organ, recent advances in neuroscience have begun to reveal more and more about its workings. However, one thing science has yet to convincingly explain is where the miracle of human consciousness comes from. Some staunchly take the view that it must be produced by the firing of neurons within the brain; others are open to explanations that do not reduce consciousness to a material process. I will not attempt to weigh up all these complex arguments here, but my views fall into that second category. I see consciousness as a fundamental force and field that pervades the Universe, and the brain is some kind of receiver and transmitter that can tune in to that field, channeling it into the particular expression known as "you."

Many scientists take similar views, comparing the brain to a radio that can be tuned to different frequencies in the spectrum of consciousness. And if the brain is a receiver, it is also a transmitter, carrying the vibrations of your thoughts and feelings out into the world, as we've discussed.

So here you are, a human being who carries around this powerful instrument for receiving and transmitting vibrations of energy. And those vibrations of energy cocreate the reality you live in, rearranging the atoms of your world in response to the frequency you're sending out. Pretty incredible, right? But if you're going to harness this power in service of your heart's desires, you need to learn how to tune the dials of that receiver/transmitter. If you're tuned in to a limited, mediocre, depressing channel, you'll cocreate a limited, mediocre, depressing life. The tool works, but the results are up to you. The Universe doesn't judge — it has given *you* the power to do that.

Most of us don't even know that there are other channels that we can tune in to. I sure didn't when I was a young man. I had my radio dial permanently set to a channel that told me that the world was scary and untrustworthy and that life was basically out to get me. As I explain in chapter 1, most people's mental and emotional radios are tuned to channels whose programming and content have been brought about by their past. Maybe the voices of their parents are speaking constantly on their private airwaves, telling them what they should do, what's possible, what life is really about. Others hear the voice of a childhood religious authority or the chatter of their own self-doubt.

If your car radio was always tuned to one channel and that channel played the same limited content day in, day out — the same boring local news, the same repetitive dull music — it would drive you crazy! Imagine how happy you'd be to discover that you had to simply turn the dial to receive access to different kinds of music, news, and information about places you'd never been to and ideas to stimulate your imagination and inspire you. Well, the same is true for your brain. There are other channels in the Universe. Even more importantly, you control the dial!

Of course, it's not as simple as just turning the dial once. Being tuned in to your limited channel has become a powerful habit, and every time you "start your car," your radio may default back to that frequency. It will take repeated tuning and retuning before you develop a new habit, which is why you need to have patience and persistence.

Finally, let's talk about your third receiver and transmitter — your heart. Did you know that your heart is in fact an electrical organ? It is by far the strongest source of bioelectricity in the body, up to sixty times stronger than the brain, which is the second-most-powerful source. Scientists have found that the heart produces an electromagnetic field that surrounds the entire body.

The heart is the most powerful broadcaster. Of all the energy senses of the body, the heart center produces the strongest signal. If we are disconnected from our heart because of fear or false beliefs, this central power source is damaged. When we transmit to the Universe, we are sending out a weak signal. Do the laws of attraction hear a weak signal? The heart broadcasts your intentions into the Universe so that the very fabric of the Universe morphs to accommodate these intentions. Emotion is the power for the broadcast. The more powerful the emotions that are attached to the intention, the more powerful the energy that the heart transmits.

Once you attune to a higher-frequency state, the heart acts like your truth meter. Run every thought through the heart. The heart knows. The thoughts of the mind can trick us. The mind can pick up unhealthy subconscious thoughts, which are really memories or past programs playing. The heart speaks in feelings, which can be more pure. Trust the heart; it has its own intelligence. The heart must work together with the brain to manifest the vibrational conditions necessary to cocreate the life of your desires. If you can create a coherent vibration between your DNA, mind, and heart, you will have access to unimaginable power.

In chapter 5, I teach you how to use these powerful instruments to receive and then transmit the particular vibration I call the Creation Frequency, and how to set this as your new default channel. This is the vibration that has given rise to everything in the Universe, and it's the vibration that you can use to cocreate the life you desire. Remember, I define the Creation Frequency as that place where your intentions and desires resonate with the intentions and desires of the Universe — that sweet spot where you are "in tune" with life. When you tap into this frequency, you will find yourself able to work in partnership with the Universe to manifest the life of your dreams.

Manifesting Money

When I sat at the mystery man's kitchen table and told him I wanted to make $10,000 a month, he didn't for a moment look surprised or disbelieving. He helped me to craft the following statement, once again following the guidelines that I would later distill into the Intention Creation Formula:

> I am so excited that my income is over $10,000 a month, and increases monthly. I love that I am able to generate this wealth doing something I love and providing great value and a joyful experience to my customers. I am so grateful for my growing paycheck and the life it makes possible for me and my family. I love my job and my career!

The powerful vibration of this intention stayed with me that night as I drove home. Not even the broken car door, the credit card bills waiting on my doorstep, or the pathetic tips at the restaurant that night could banish the positive feeling I got when I closed my eyes and recalled those words. Perhaps there was something to this after all.

4

From Fear to Love

WEEK FOUR

Love is what we were born with. Fear is what we have learned here.
The spiritual journey is the relinquishment — or unlearning —
of fear and the acceptance of love back into our hearts.

— Marianne Williamson, *A Return to Love*

A week later, I was still feeling pretty upbeat as I arrived at the mystery man's house for my next session. The sun was shining, so at least my arm was warm as it held the car door shut. Keeping in mind my intention to own my own business had made going to the restaurant every day a little easier. As I waited tables and bussed dishes, I'd been thinking about what my next intention would be.

One word kept coming back to me: *home*. I wanted a home — a place that was truly mine, where I could put down roots and watch my kids grow. It didn't have to be a big fancy house, but it would be lovingly cared for and welcoming. It would be a lot nicer than the house of the man who was supposed to teach me how to get it, I thought with a wry smile, as I knocked on the door of his humble abode.

When we were seated at the kitchen table, paper and pencil at the ready, I told the mystery man about my intention to own a home.

"Home," he repeated. "It's a powerful word. A home is much more than a physical place — a house or an apartment. A home is shaped by the emotions of those who inhabit it. To write an effective intention to own a home, you will need to infuse it with the positive emotions that a home represents to you. But when you speak about home, I'm sensing a lot of different vibrations around that idea. I sense love, but I also sense fear. Tell me about the home you grew up in."

Closing my eyes, I could picture it. The 1960s suburban Cincinnati neighborhood packed with newly built homes, just a few feet apart. Inside, white walls and modern furnishings. The two-car garage with the basketball hoop in front that my dad had put up.

"Now, tell me how it felt," he probed.

As I recalled my childhood, I couldn't pull a coherent answer from the confusing tangle of emotions that arose. Finally, I told him, "There were two different homes. One when my father was away on his business trips, and one when he returned." My dad was a hard-working salesman who taught me to always give 150 percent — "If you're going to do something, do it right" was one of his favorite sayings. But he was also an alcoholic. When

Dad was gone, our house was full of fun, laughter, board games, and dinner on the table at six, and my mom was happy, loving, and attentive. When he was home, dinner was rarely on the table before eight. He would get home from work at six, and Mom's attention would be immediately on him. They would drink for a few hours, which sometimes gave rise to great humor and frivolity and other times to angry outbursts. My childhood oscillated on a weekly basis between normalcy and chaos. Oftentimes, when I opened our front door, I didn't know which home I was entering until I'd crossed the threshold.

The mystery man was quiet when I finished my description. Finally, he looked at me with eyes full of kindness, and said, "Love and fear. Both of these powerful emotions shaped your childhood, and both of them still live within you. If you are to be successful in manifesting your heart's desires, the force of love within you needs to become stronger than the force of fear."

He explained that fear is the greatest obstacle to our ability to tune in to the powerful energy of love — fear that has been programmed into us since childhood; fear that arises from our past wounds and betrayals; fear that we are inadequate, incapable, or unworthy. "When you talked about home, I could sense that fear still has a grip on your heart," he explained. "As we write your intention today, we need to focus on love. Love is what channels the energy of your intention toward positive outcomes."

This was a critical lesson. We'd spoken before about infusing intentions with emotion, but now he was pointing me toward the most powerful emotion, love, and its counterforce, fear. Later, I found this idea repeated in the writings and teachings of many of the great masters of manifestation.

What's Love Got to Do with It?

The visionary author Neale Donald Walsch writes, "There are only two energies at the core of the human experience: love and fear."[1] In one of my favorite books, *Love Is Letting Go of Fear*, Gerald G. Jampolsky echoes this idea: "There are only two emotions: one is Love and the other is fear. Love is our true reality. Fear is something our mind has made up, and is therefore unreal."[2]

I like this way of looking at life. Of course, there are so many different complex emotions we feel, but at a primal level, these two forces — love and fear — shape much of our lives. We all come into this world as innocent little beings of energy and love. But at some point, we are wounded, betrayed, let down. We begin downloading information from our parents, our teachers, our environment, the media, and the society we live in. We learn to protect ourselves, we learn not to trust, and we learn to be afraid. Some of us never find our way back from fear to love, but some of us are lucky enough to be offered the opportunity to rediscover the love and innocence that is our original nature.

This was the deeper spiritual journey that I was embarking on as I set out to manifest the life of my dreams, although I didn't really know it at the time. I was beginning the task of freeing myself from the fear that my difficult childhood had engraved in my cells. What the mystery man intuitively knew is that love always vibrates at a higher frequency than fear. The way to free yourself from fear is to focus on love.

Another person who deeply understood the role of love as a central principle of the law of attraction was Charles F. Haanel, an early twentieth-century writer known as "the father of personal development." Haanel was a major inspiration for the movie *The Secret*, and his book *The Master Key System*, originally published more than a century ago as a twenty-four-part correspondence course, remains one of the definitive works on the principles of manifestation. It was formative for the great Napoleon Hill, and legend has it that Bill Gates read and was influenced by the book while at college. Haanel taught, "It is the combination of Thought and Love which forms the irresistible force, called the law of attraction." Expanding on this idea, he wrote:

> The principle which gives thought the dynamic power to correlate with its object, and therefore to master every adverse human experience, is the law of attraction, which is another name for love. This is an eternal and fundamental principle, inherent in all things, in every system of Philosophy, in every Religion, and in every Science. There is no getting away from the law of love. It

is feeling that imparts vitality to thought. Feeling is desire, and desire is love. Thought impregnated with love becomes invincible.[3]

Haanel recognized that the force he was teaching people to harness was intimately connected to the fabric of the entire Universe. He wrote, "The law of love is the creative force behind every manifestation, not only of atoms, but of worlds, of the Universe, of everything of which the imagination can form any conception."[4]

I've come to understand that love is much more than an emotion you feel toward people you care about. It truly is a cosmic force. The poet Dante described "the Love which moves the sun and the other stars."[5] Love is fundamental to the workings of the Universe. "The universe only pretends to be made of matter. Secretly, it is made of love,"[6] author Daniel Pinchbeck recently wrote on Twitter.

When it comes to cosmic forces, who better to describe them than a cosmologist? Brian Swimme writes beautifully about love as a cosmic principle in his book *The Universe Is a Green Dragon*. "Love begins as allurement — as attraction. Think of the entire cosmos, all one hundred billion galaxies rushing through space: At this cosmic scale, the basic dynamism of the universe is the attraction each galaxy has for every other galaxy." He even suggests that what we call *gravity* is actually synonymous with love, in the cosmic sense: "Gravity is the word we use to *point* to this primary attraction, but no matter how intelligently we theorize about the *consequences* of this attraction, the actual attracting activity remains a mystery."[7]

Describing how this plays out at both a molecular and a human level, he writes, "The proton is attracted only to certain particles. On an infinitely more complex level, the same holds true for humans: Each person discovers a field of allurements, the totality of which bears the unique stamp of that person's personality. Destiny unfolds in the pursuit of individual fascinations and interests....By pursuing your allurements, you help bind the universe together. The unity of the world rests on the pursuit of passion."[8]

Swimme uses the term *allurement* where I might use *intention* or *desire*, but the principle is the same: Intention and love are two elemental forces that come together to form the vibration of the Creation Frequency. It's the vibration that gave rise to everything you see. It doesn't really matter whether you believe that creativity and intention come from God or from a process called evolution — either way, its power for generating novelty and beauty is breathtaking. And it is inseparable from your own essential nature — you are both a product and an instrument of that creativity and intention. When you begin to tune in to the Creation Frequency, you become like a member of the cosmic orchestra — playing your unique part in harmony with the greater whole.

Intention is simply the desire to create — that elemental drive that turns possibility into reality, whether it's the new car you want or a whole Universe made out of nothing. Intention is another way of describing the creative power of consciousness, the energy that exists at the heart of life and keeps it growing. Love is what attunes that intention toward the highest and most positive outcomes.

Accessing the Creation Frequency involves tuning in to the cosmic energies of intention and love that flow through the Universe and through your own consciousness, and then channeling them into your particular human desires and passions in order to transmit them out into the Universe. As I've explained, the Universe doesn't judge — it will give you whatever you desire — but if your desire and intention are connected to love, they will manifest faster because love is the energy that binds the Universe.

A Home Filled with Love

Home. Sitting at the mystery man's table, I brought my attention back to that word and tried to fill it with the energy of love. Together we wrote the following intention:

> I love that I own a beautiful home. It is so alive
> with an open-door policy so that dear friends and
> family are always welcome. We have so much fun
> here! What a beautiful bond our family is form-
> ing, based on love and support. I am blessed that
> our home was easy to buy with no money down
> and that the monthly payments are so affordable.

I relish the beautiful rose bushes and other flowers, and I especially enjoy the lush green grass. Owning my own home makes me feel so accomplished and wonderful. I am grateful for this inspiring place in which my family can grow and thrive for many years to come.

As I drove slowly back through the suburban streets, I tried to picture this house just around the corner, on the next block, over the hill. I held on to the image in my mind even as the streets grew rougher, the green lawns gave way to dirty sidewalks, and apartment blocks replaced the little family homes. After parking the car, I walked back to my lonely, rented one-bedroom apartment. It could not have been further from the home I'd envisioned, but when I closed my eyes, I could still feel the warmth, the joy, and the power of love.

5

Raise Your Frequency

WEEK FIVE

He who lives in harmony with himself
lives in harmony with the universe.

— Marcus Aurelius

It had been a tough week. My last session with the mystery man had brought to the surface many painful memories from childhood. Evoking the love-filled home I wanted to create had only made me more aware of how lonely I was. Lisa wouldn't return my calls and I hadn't seen my daughter. Working double shifts, I'd barely slept. Whenever my head hit the pillow, I was tormented by the fear that I'd never get my family back and all of this effort was for nothing. Would little Michelle even remember who I was if she didn't see me every day? How long would it be before Lisa found someone else — a nice guy with a good job and no problems, who would take care of her in the way she deserved? Maybe I should just get the hell out of here, leave town, and start fresh somewhere else. The old, familiar urge to run away grew stronger every night as I tossed and turned, fighting a cold and craving a drink. I hadn't broken my promise to quit alcohol and drugs, but I felt like I was hanging by a thread.

On the day I was supposed to meet the mystery man, I almost drove right past his street. There was a bar just a few blocks away, and my $50 would buy enough drinks to make me forget about everything, at least for a few hours. At the last minute, however, I slammed on the brakes, made the turn, and pulled up to his driveway. I wasn't going to quit now, not when I was so close to completing the seven weeks and receiving the mysterious gift he had promised.

When he opened the door, he didn't say a word, just handed me a cup of coffee he'd already poured. I was no longer surprised that he seemed to know my state of mind before I said a word.

Pouring a second cup for himself, he sat down and said, "Okay, before we get to your next intention, there are some things we need to talk about."

I was itching to get to the seventh week and learn the mysterious secret — you probably are, too. But there was another important step that had to be taken first. The mystery man explained to me that in order for my desires to manifest, it was important to bring my life into alignment — to make sure I was living with basic integrity. "What that means," he explained, "is that you need to be taking care of the instruments through which your intentions will manifest — your body, mind, heart, and soul. Imagine being in perfect balance with the Universe, resonating harmoniously in a profound state of relaxation."

His tone was gentle but his next words cut to the point. "Look at you — you're a mess. How is the Universe supposed to work with you and through you if your body is barely functioning, your mind is consumed with anxiety, your heart is full of pain, and your soul is starved for meaning?"

Living in Congruency

Creating integrity is a step that too many manifestation teachings skip over, and I believe it's one of the reasons so many of them fail to provide satisfying results for the people who try them.

If you don't like the word *integrity* (perhaps it reminds you of Sunday school or moralizing lectures from a parent or teacher), then how about *congruency*? I'm not going to preach to you about how you should live — but I will tell you that the Universe is very sensitive to congruency. This is a critical piece if you want to be successful in manifesting your deepest desires. If you're living in a way that is fragmented or contradictory, if your loyalties are divided between conflicting priorities, if you're enslaved by unconscious fears or unacknowledged doubts, you'll struggle to become a powerful cocreator. If you're neglecting to take care of your own body and soul, you may sabotage yourself before you've even begun. So before we move into the manifestation techniques, let's take a moment to ensure that you are in alignment. If you're not, this chapter will inspire you to begin moving in that direction.

Returning to the metaphor I use in chapter 3, this process is similar to the tuning of the orchestra so that the instruments can play in harmony. Your thoughts, emotions, and actions need to be essentially attuned to one another if your life is to make beautiful music.

The process of alignment is not some major project you need to undertake before you can begin. This is not about perfection or meeting some externally imposed moral standard. It is a self-directed process that will be ongoing throughout your creation journey as you fine-tune your power to design your own reality. The Creation Frequency is not a one-way delivery system for your desires. It's not a letter to Santa Claus that you send up the chimney and then wait for the morning delivery. It's a cocreative process in which you work *with* the Universe. Keeping your life in alignment is one of the ways that you fulfill your part of this collaboration — ensuring that the conditions are optimal for the realization of your dreams. At the beginning of your journey, we're going to focus on three areas:

1. Shifting from the head to the heart
2. Taking care of the body
3. Nourishing the spirit

The Longest Journey Is
from the Head to the Heart

As I've explained, most of us have been programmed since childhood to live out of fear. We've also been programmed to live in our heads — the place where the negative programming was installed. The head feels safer because thoughts don't hurt like feelings do, but in the head we are imprisoned by illusions. The most important journey a human being makes is only about a foot long — from the head to the heart. The heart is where love lives. It's where we naturally lived when we were small children, before the fear set in. In that place, everything is possible, and we cannot fail.

As we grow up in this confusing and frightening world, most of us slowly shift into our heads because we're given the message that our heads are the safest places to be. We end up doing everything backward. The system keeps us in our heads, which is where we are susceptible to societal programming. This makes us suffer, but we continue to use our heads to try and think our way out of the uncomfortable places we find ourselves in rather than tapping into the desires of our hearts and allowing those desires to guide us.

We — especially men — are programmed not to feel. We've been told it is not safe to feel painful emotions and not appropriate to express our deeper feelings. Our whole central nervous system is based on feelings, and yet we are taught to ignore them. Imagine what is accessible when we allow ourselves the simple act of feeling. That's why we need to make that foot-long journey — the most important journey we ever make — back to our hearts.

In the heart, a desire arises to create — to create a better life for ourselves and others. The heart brings us back into balance, creating congruency in our lives. Once we're grounded there, we can use the mind the way it was meant to be used: as a tool to formulate plans, create strategies, and gather resources to manifest the desires of our hearts.

When we move from the head to the heart, the fearful mind begins to lose power, and the power of the heart is free to fully blossom. Then we are free to truly love and create. True love evolves into service — the expression of universal love.

Take Care of Your Body: Your Spirit's Temple

It's critical to nurture and honor the body that houses your essence or spirit. The more you take care of your trillions of cells, the more available you will be to live, love, and give. If you are not taking care of the needs of your body, your attention will not be free to even become aware of the needs of the other parts of your being — of your mind, your heart, or your soul — let alone of the needs of others. You might be the most spiritual person ever born on this Earth, but if your body is sick, tired, or overweight, you won't be able to do anything more than sit on the couch.

Here are the basics (as I understand them) when it comes to the practical matter of taking care of the body. First, give the body an alkaline diet, which means a diet that is primarily composed of living, organic, plant-based foods. Second, remember that your body is 60 to 65 percent water, and keep it replenished (high-pH water is best, with 9.5 pH being optimal for the body). Third, it's important to move. Tony Robbins says, "If you want to change your life, move your body! It generates energy."

Here's one of my favorite ways to raise your frequency — get out and move in nature. Hike, run, or do whatever activity you prefer. Leave your cell phone at home, so it's just you and nature. You'll nourish your body *and* your spirit. Some people find it easiest to connect with their inner self when surrounded by a beautiful environment. Taking walks in the wilderness or simply sitting quietly in a forest, by a lake, on a hilltop, or at a beach can become a setting for journeying within and accessing your essential nature. Nature's grandeur has a way of lifting us out of our limited self-definitions and quieting our chattering minds. It helps us connect with the deeper forces that created all that beauty and us as well. Even visiting a city park in the middle of your day, or taking a slow walk around your neighborhood in the evening, can help you focus on the natural sounds behind the human ones.

Nourish the Spirit

You don't have to adhere to a spiritual or religious faith to master the Creation Frequency. But if you accept the amazing truths that science has revealed to us, which I share in chapter 3, you will recognize a deeper dimension to consciousness and to life, a dimension where you discover the essence of who you are. I use the term *spiritual* to point to this dimension of existence, and it's important to nourish this part of yourself if you want to raise your frequency.

To connect with your own spirit, you need to get still and quiet, in whatever way works for you, so that you can sink into a deeper dimension of consciousness. Who are you? Are you the physical body that was born on a certain day in a certain place to your specific parents? Are you the name they gave you? Are you the particular personality that has emerged over time, with its quirks, its strengths, its likes and dislikes? Are you the psychological wounds and scars that life and other people have inflicted upon you? Are you the hard-won wisdom that came out of those difficult times? Are you the fears and prejudices you've learned from culture, or the achievements and possessions you have accumulated? Yes, you may be all of these things, but they are not the deepest part of who you are. Beneath these surface characteristics is a deeper or more essential self that some might call your *soul* or *true self*. You need to connect with that self in order to activate the Creation Frequency.

I grew up Catholic, and I have found great spiritual

support through attending Mass as an adult during certain times in my life. For a short period, I was a born-again Christian. These days, I don't belong to any particular denomination, but I practice elements of both Christianity and Buddhism. Based on everything I've learned, I have certain beliefs, and the most fundamental one is that we are all connected. I believe that at the heart of every religion is this same message. I hear a fundamental unity of wisdom beneath their different myths, methods, and mysteries. They tell us that God is love, they tell us to serve others, and they tell us that we are all one.

You can nourish the spirit in many ways, and it's important to choose those that resonate for you. If you already have a religious faith or spiritual practice, you may find nourishment there. Prayer, meditation, contemplation, and other ancient spiritual arts can all be powerful sources of connection. Spending time in the beauty of the natural world nourishes the spirit just as it nourishes the body. Other ways to connect to this dimension of life include playing with children, being with loved ones, hugs, laughter, yoga, serving others, and engaging in any activity that you love so much it makes time stop, absorbing you in the present moment.

One important way that I nourish my spirit is reflected on my bookshelf. All my life, I have been fascinated by religion and spirituality, by life and death, by the fundamental question "Why are we here?" I spend time every day reading or listening to audiobooks by some of the greatest spiritual visionaries, both past and present.

My reading list over the years has included the Bible, the Koran, the Bhagavad Gita, and many Buddhist texts, as well as books by contemporary spiritual teachers like Eckhart Tolle, Byron Katie, and Ram Dass, and self-help masters like Tony Robbins and Jack Canfield.

Whatever you choose as your personal pathway to spirit, be sure to give it time and space in your life. A well-nourished spirit activates your life force and makes you a clear transmitter to the Universe.

Creation Frequency Journaling

One simple practice I find to be not only spiritually nourishing but helpful in measuring and adjusting my intentions is daily journaling. For most of my life, I have kept a journal, and I value having a record of my life that I can periodically look back over, reflecting on the things that I struggled with and overcame, along with my many blessings. I try to take quiet time every morning to write in my journal. My approach is very simple. It has three steps: I begin with gratitude, ask for wisdom, and end with love.

1. **Express Gratitude:** I start by thanking God or the Universe for all the things in my life that I am grateful for having cocreated. I tap into the vibration of this powerful emotion. Gratitude opens

the heart and connects you to the energy of love and abundance. I acknowledge all that is currently manifesting in my life in alignment with the intentions I have created. This practice highlights the quality and quantity of the intentions that have already manifested and increases faith that the process is working, in big and small ways. I address my gratitude to the Creator, but you will find the form that feels most authentic for your own expression.

2. Ask for Wisdom: I believe that there is a field of energy and intelligence in the Universe that can help me find guidance in my life. I ask for wisdom in navigating whatever choices, challenges, or dilemmas face me. I write down each specific situation, which helps to invite in the wisdom and focus the energy of the Universe on that particular issue. In this way, I actively participate in removing subconscious blocks so that my intentions can manifest more quickly. As you journal, you will find the words that help to open your heart to receive the wisdom of the Universe.

3. Offer Love: I end by offering thanks and love to the power and energy that connects us all. Remember, love is the most powerful emotion. The vibration of love radiates out from my heart into my immediate surroundings, to the people I love, and into the Universe. Increasing the frequency of love in my heart allows me to be a more powerful transmitter of my intentions and have a greater positive impact in the world.

Some days my entries are short; some days they are long. I spend about ten minutes journaling each day, followed by about five minutes just sitting and being quiet. I find this keeps me connected with my own spiritual nature and with the greater spiritual reality that I am part of.

Tony Robbins often says a life worth living is a life worth recording. Periodically reread your journal. Go back and highlight every miracle that has happened in your life. This is a great practice for establishing proof in the subconscious mind that the Creation Frequency does indeed work. It will help you carry on through the challenging times. It will also help you observe patterns and figure out why you get stuck and how to free yourself up.

Synchronicity

When your life starts to become more congruent, you may begin to experience the amazing power that is sometimes called *synchronicity*, a word coined in the 1950s by Carl Gustav Jung to describe "meaningful coincidences." Have you ever opened a book randomly to find the exact advice you need jumping off the page? Or have you struck up a conversation with a stranger in the line at the grocery store only to find that he or she is exactly the person who can help you achieve an important goal? You may dismiss these as mere acts of randomness, but Jung believed that such events give us a glimpse into the underlying order of the Universe, demonstrating what he called the "acausal connecting principle" linking mind and matter.

When you bring your life into alignment, you become more in tune with the harmony of life, more open to that "connecting principle." As spiritual teacher and author Deepak Chopra writes, "Once you understand the way life really works — the flow of energy, information, and intelligence that directs every moment — then you begin to see the amazing potential in that moment.... You also begin to encounter more and more coincidences in your life."[1]

I've found this to be true — and such coincidences are anything but accidents. Synchronicity is the Universe's way of affirming that you are coming into deeper alignment. You may not be able to see the connection between cause and effect, but that doesn't mean it's not there. Pay attention as these events become more common in your life — it will give you confidence that you are on the right path.

The Energy of Health

As the mystery man explained to me the importance of bringing my life into alignment, it became clear to me what my next intention would be. How could I achieve all the things I'd described so far without a strong and healthy body?

Together, we crafted the following statement of my intention to achieve optimal health:

I cherish how healthy I am and how great I feel.
I love how I look in the mirror: perfect body weight, lean and mean! I feel powerful as I effortlessly jog and run, especially during a marathon.
I am grateful for the endorphin release that makes my thinking clearer and brighter. I fully receive the extra oxygen intake as it purifies my blood and my organs. I love how I feel: powerful, strong, clear, vibrant, and ready to embrace life to the fullest!

That night, when I got home, I looked in the mirror, noticing how out of shape I was. My diet of fast food from the restaurants where I waited tables wasn't doing me any favors. I pulled on shorts and sneakers and went for a run around my neighborhood. I'd barely gone two blocks before I was out of breath, stopping to clutch my side and cough. Clearly, I was far from the picture of health that my statement described, but I tried to recall the feelings anyway — to override the immediate experience of weakness and pain with the sensations of strength, energy, and confidence. Taking a deep breath, I started running again. One foot, then the other. Breathe in, breathe out.

6 The Power of Giving

WEEK SIX

I slept and I dreamed that life is all joy.
I woke and I saw that life is all service.
I served and I saw that service is joy.

— Rabindranath Tagore

"This will be your final intention," the mystery man told me when I showed up for my session during the sixth week. "What do you still want to create?"

I drew a blank. I'd already gone through all my significant dreams — getting back my wife and daughter, owning my own business, increasing my income, buying a house, improving my health. If all of those came true, I'd achieve more than I could ever have hoped for.

"There's nothing more I want," I told him. "Can we just move ahead to the secret you were going to show me?"

"Your intentions don't all have to be about getting,"

he replied. "What about an intention to give? What can you do to help others, to make the world a better place?"

I must confess, at that stage in my life, this was not a question I'd ever given much thought. Most of the time I seemed to have too many problems of my own to be thinking about other people's problems. And what did I have to offer, anyway? I was a mess. I couldn't even get my own life together. I was embarrassed to admit this to the mystery man, but then it occurred to me that he probably already knew it — he always seemed to be one step ahead. Sure enough, he smiled and said, "I know you don't think you have much to give, and you may not have really considered helping others, but deep down I think you care more than you realize. Think about a time when the suffering of someone else touched you."

I was quiet. "Take your time," he added. "Listen to your heart. Trust that the answer is there."

We sat in silence for several minutes, and then a memory arose. I was sitting with my father, during one of his rare moments of sobriety, and he was telling me stories of his own difficult childhood — how his parents had both been alcoholics, and he'd eventually been made a ward of the state. He ended up in juvenile hall, and then his aunt came and got him out and raised him. She really changed his life. I was only a child myself at the time, but I remember feeling like my heart would burst. The same feeling came back a couple of years later when I watched a documentary about a Catholic priest who created homes for troubled teenage boys.

"There it is," the mystery man said, and I looked up, surprised, not realizing he'd been watching me intently. "You connected. That feeling is the key to your final intention. Don't worry about how you're going to find the extra time, money, or energy. Just focus on your feeling of caring and connection to other people. That's what compassion is — the feeling of caring that occurs when our conscious awareness senses our true interrelationship with everyone and everything else in the Universe. Keep your attention on what moves you and describe how you're going to make a difference."

I didn't ask any more questions, just followed his instructions. I was eager to get this last intention written, so I'd be one step closer to the seventh week, when he would fulfill his promise and give me the mysterious gift that would help make all these intentions into reality. What I didn't realize was that this sixth intention was in and of itself a powerful gift. Only many years later did I understand that telling me to give may have been the most important thing the mystery man ever said to me.

Becoming a Giver

What does it mean to become a giver? Many of us tend to have an idea of what giving means — donating a lot of money to charity or volunteering a lot of time to help those less fortunate. We may feel guilty that we don't live up to that ideal, or we look forward to the day when we are no longer so busy trying to make ends meet that we have the extra money and free time to do so. However, too often, if we put off giving for some future day, it can blind us to what we could be giving right now. As Irish politician and philosopher Edmund Burke wrote, "Nobody makes a greater mistake than he who did nothing because he could only do a little."

The idea that we don't have enough right now to give anything to others is a powerful mindset. Most of us have grown up in a culture fueled by the unconscious conviction that there's not enough to go around. So we feel driven to get as much as we can for ourselves and hold on to it — whether it be money, possessions, time, love, or attention. Of course, far too many people in this world live in conditions of actual scarcity, and you may be one of them. I'm not suggesting that anyone should deny their real needs or those of their family. But for many more of us, scarcity is more a mindset than an actual condition. We're convinced something is "missing," and if we could just fill that void, we'd be free to give to others. "We live with scarcity as an underlying assumption," writes Lynne Twist in *The Soul of Money*.[1] She points out the telling fact that this mindset of "not enough" and "more is better" afflicts the rich as much as it does the poor. That kind of void can never be filled by more possessions.

This mindset is hard to dislodge. By numerous measures, the standard of living in the United States has clearly risen over the past fifty years. But are we happier? It seems to me that the cultural craving for more has not lessened at all. And even those who have more than enough money feel the lack of other things just as acutely. I know plenty of millionaires who are miserable, still seeking to fill that hole in the soul.

What I discovered, as have many others, is that the only way to fill that void is to stop trying and to go in the completely opposite direction. Start giving. If you don't have money to spare, give of your time. Give your knowledge — share what you've learned or discovered with others. Give someone your full attention for the duration of a conversation. Give a smile to a stranger when you don't really feel like it. You can become a giver in countless ways and discover the abundance of love that flows through your life when you replace a mindset of scarcity with one of generosity.

The Purpose of Life Is to Serve

When you become a giver, you stumble upon the beautiful truth that the mystery man tried to teach me, all those years ago: Meaning is found in the act of giving. The quickest way to get out of grief, pain, despair, or anything that troubles you is simply to give. It's easy to be lost in your own suffering, until you meet someone who is in a worse situation than you are. Believe me, if you sincerely try, you can always find someone worse off than you. There's an old saying: "I used to think I was badly off because I had no shoes, until I met a man who had no feet." When you're feeling like life is hard and you're getting a raw deal, try thinking about another person and their problems rather than your own.

The purpose of life is to serve. This is by no means a new discovery — in fact, it is a theme we can trace back through many of the great religious and humanist traditions. "For it is in giving that we receive," said Saint Francis of Assisi in his prayer "Make Me an Instrument of Your Peace." It's also an insight that is supported by modern psychology. A 2012 Stanford University study investigated happiness and meaning among four hundred Americans aged eighteen to seventy-eight, and the study concluded that for participants "meaningfulness went with being a giver rather than a taker."[2] I humbly offer my own experience and perspective on this simple but powerful realization, along with some of the stories, writings, and insights that have most inspired me, in the hope that they may inspire others to embrace a life of giving.

Many of us have been brought up to pursue happiness, as our Founding Fathers decreed. But happiness is a highly subjective and elusive state, one that tends to slip from our grasp when pursued for its own sake. As Holocaust survivor Viktor Frankl, author of the classic *Man's Search for Meaning*, wrote, "It is the very pursuit of happiness that thwarts happiness."[3] Frankl, who chose to stay in his native Vienna to care for his parents rather than escape, was sent to a concentration camp, where he lost his entire family, including his pregnant wife. He went through more suffering than most of us can imagine, but he came out the other side with an extraordinary perspective on what it takes to live a meaningful life. He found meaning in what we can contribute, to others or to the world. He wrote, "A man who becomes conscious of the responsibility he bears toward a human being who affectionately waits for him, or to an unfinished work... knows the 'why' for his existence and will be able to bear almost any 'how.'"[4]

Happiness, Frankl concluded, "cannot be pursued; it must ensue." In other words, happiness is a by-product of living a purposeful and meaningful life. He also wrote, "Being human always points, and is directed, to something or someone other than oneself.... The more one forgets himself — by giving himself to a cause to serve or another person to love — the more human he is."[5] A meaningful life, as the Stanford study confirms, comes from being a giver.

You Can't Out-Give God

If, instead of taking, you start giving — be it money, time, work, or simply love, availability, and attention — you may notice a surprising result, that you start filling up. This is sometimes called "the law of reciprocity," and I believe it's as much a part of how our Universe works as the law of gravity. It simply states that what you freely give, with a loving heart, comes back to you, multiplied.

This sentiment is expressed beautifully by many great spiritual and motivational teachers, including Zig Ziglar, whose seminar I attended in 1980 before I even met the mystery man. I remember him sharing his now-well-known saying, "You can have everything you want in life if you help enough other people get what they want." The same basic idea can be found in many places in the Bible. "Give and it will be given to you," says Luke (6:38). I like this version of the message from 2 Corinthians 9:6–8:

> Whoever sows generously will also reap generously. Each man should give what he has decided in his heart to give, not reluctantly or under compulsion, for God loves a cheerful giver. And God is able to make all grace abound to you, so that in all things at all times, having all that you need, you will abound in every good work.

Another way I've heard it put is "you can't out-give God." If you're not comfortable with that term, substitute *the Universe* instead — the principle remains the same. No matter how much you give, more will come back to you. The only caveat is that you have to give with a pure heart, out of love — not out of duty, obligation, or a desire for anything in return.

The purpose of life is to serve. Don't wait to start giving until you feel you have enough or are good enough. Start today, right now, with an open and compassionate heart. Give love, give kindness, give a smile, or simply give your attention. It will come back to you one hundredfold.

Ideally, when you start to create the life of your dreams, build the act of giving into the intentions you set for yourself. Don't let it be an afterthought or a by-product of the wealth and success you intend to have one day; make it part of your definition of success. This way you will ensure a life of meaning and purpose.

Once again, service doesn't have to mean contributing money or effort to a particular cause. Sometimes service comes down to simply being available to another person, giving them your full attention. This is really the essence of what it means to be a giver. It means making yourself available for moments like that. How many opportunities do you miss every day to make that kind of difference? It might take as little as a smile or a kind gesture to change another person's day, or even to change their life.

We never know what impact our simple acts of kindness and availability can have. As you go through your daily life, experiment with giving just a little more of your attention to the people you interact with. Leave aside your own thoughts, worries, and frustrations as you interact with the checkout person at the grocery store or with a client or colleague. Do so for the space of a meal shared with family or friends. Notice how much of the time you are distracted and not fully present. Take a risk to leave all those nagging thoughts aside. Don't worry —if they're important, they'll still be there when you are done giving your attention to someone else.

A Promise Made

I did not understand any of this when the mystery man instructed me to write my sixth intention. All I had was that feeling in my heart that had awoken when I remembered listening to my father's stories of his troubled childhood. So I took that feeling and turned it into the following statement:

> It is deeply rewarding to have created a transformational facility that serves as a home for troubled youth. I feel so purposeful knowing that I am helping young people who are struggling like my dad when he was growing up. I am able to draw on my own experience to share the wisdom, strength, and hope I have gained in turning my life around. It is so uplifting to share the twelve steps with these young men. I am so grateful to be of service!

That was the promise I put out to the Universe. And although, at the time, I didn't really know what it meant, or how important it was, it felt good to write it. In fact, it felt better than any of the statements I had written about what I wanted for myself. As I drove away that day, it was as if, for a brief moment, I'd been lifted above the cares and fears of my life. I stopped obsessing over the mistakes of my past, and for the first time in weeks, I wasn't thinking about the future. I wasn't even anticipating the following week, when the mysterious gift would finally be revealed. In that moment, I was able to simply *be*.

7

The Mystery Man's Gift

WEEK SEVEN

As a man thinketh in his heart, so is he.
— James Allen, *As a Man Thinketh*

"You've been here a while," the mystery man commented when he opened the door. "You should have come in." *Had he looked out the window and seen the car?* I wondered. The drapes in front were all closed. *Or did he just know?*

I had indeed arrived early for my seventh and final session. I'd sat in the car drumming my fingernails against the steering wheel, counting the minutes until it was time to knock on the door. I did not really know what to expect, but I was nervous and excited. The gift that the mystery man had been promising was within reach — the one that would turn all my carefully crafted intentions into reality.

He had asked me to bring all of my written intentions,

and now I spread them out on the table in front of me — six pieces of paper that captured my heart's deepest longings. The mystery man read each one, silently, and then he said, "You're ready. Now you're going to learn how to creatively send and receive the necessary energy to make your life vision come true in the outer world." With that, he left the room.

When he returned, he was carrying two cassette players and a blank tape. Many younger readers may have never used this antiquated technology, but older readers will remember when such things were the state of the art.

"Today," the mystery man explained, "we are going to create the transmitter that will carry your intentions out into the universe. This is the gift I promised you. If you create this transmitter according to my instructions, and you play it every day, your dreams cannot help but come true."

Before I continue, let me reassure you that my method for creating the transmitter no longer involves cassettes. I'll teach you how to do this for yourself in a moment, but first, here is the story of how the mystery man and I created that first transmitter, using the best technology available at the time.

The mystery man started a prerecorded tape on the first cassette player, and hypnotic music filled the kitchen. He explained that this music would play in the background while I read my intentions aloud and made a recording using the blank tape in the second cassette player. First, however, I needed to record some instructions for relaxation; later, when I listened to the tape, I would follow these instructions before hearing my intentions. He handed me a script to read — the same "Relaxation Script" I use today (see pages 121–23). Slowly, I read the script aloud, followed by my six intentions, and these were recorded with the music in the background. The mystery man told me that I should listen to that cassette tape every morning and night.

Now that you understand the principles underlying the Creation Frequency, you are empowered and ready to learn the process for manifesting your specific desires. This process is exactly what the mystery man taught me all those decades ago, although the process as I now practice it has been enhanced with modern technology.

Choose Your Intentions

I hope that as you've read this book, you've been practicing by writing your own intentions following the Intention Creation Formula (see chapter 2). By now, you may have lots of intentions or just a few. Before you can begin the process of creating your transmitter, you need to select the intentions that you plan to work on. I recommend that you choose no more than six to begin with. Ideally, to create a balanced life vision, I suggest that you create one intention for each of the six categories in "The Six Categories of Desire" (see the boxed text, pages 114–15). These categories represent, to me, a holistic view of human life. To some extent, it's natural that we will focus more on one dimension or another at different times in our lives, but if we neglect any of these key areas, we may find ourselves out of balance and unfulfilled, even if we get all the things we thought we wanted.

If you have not already done so, craft a powerful statement for each of your six intentions, following the Intention Creation Formula (see page 33). Take your time. Come back to them each day until you feel them vibrating and resonating with the energy of your heart and soul. Remember what the mystery man said — they should be "a vibrant, multisensory life vision of what you truly want." Read them aloud to yourself. Once you can see and feel your intentions powerfully, they are already beginning to take shape in the unseen world of possibility. It is only a matter of time until the atoms rearrange themselves and you see your desire manifest itself in the physical dimension. Remember: The closer your intentions vibrate to the frequency of love and compassion, the faster they will materialize.

In this book, you may notice that the six original intentions I created with the mystery man apply to only five of the categories of desire. I neglected to create an intention for "Personal and Spiritual Development." Today, I give much more attention to this dimension of my life. Here's an example of my current intention in this regard:

I am a powerful spiritual being having a physical human experience. I have ecstatic continuous access to my Creator. I intentionally employ the many valuable spiritual tools I have in my tool-box, which uplift me further each day. I love how my heart sings when I am one with nature and one with everything. I feel empowered by my Creator to be the fullest expression of myself so that I can serve the greatest good. I love my life!

Finally, before confirming your choices, take a moment to ask yourself whether your intentions are aligned with one another. Does the future you are envisioning have integrity and balance? Reread your intentions for each of the six areas, and then ask yourself: Will these harmoniously coexist? Or am I setting up contradictory desires?

For example, if your relationships and family goal is about having a baby, and your career goal is to start a new business, those might not both be able to happen at the same time. Remember, ask these questions not to raise doubts about whether your goals are attainable — simply look for areas that might be in conflict with one another. Doing this will ensure that you are taking a balanced and holistic approach to the life you intend to live, and you are not setting yourself up for problems down the road. One of the most common areas in which I see this happen is when our goals related to career, vocation, money, and material possessions demand so much of us that they eclipse our goals in other areas of life.

I let this happen to me when I began my cocreation journey. You may have noticed that in my sessions with the mystery man, many of my intentions focused on the material dimension of life — understandable, perhaps, for a young man, but not ideal. In fact, after I completed my work with the mystery man, I allowed those goals to be so all-consuming that my sixth intention — the promise to be of service — slipped out of sight for many years. I'll return to that story and the lesson it taught me in the next chapter — for now, I encourage you to seek balance in your own life vision.

When you read your list of intentions, you should feel the harmonious vibration of a balanced and integrated life. If one element feels out of tune with the rest, you may want to think about how to adjust your intentions so that they work better together. Again, this is not necessarily about pulling back or scaling down your intentions. Don't allow your fears and doubts to hijack this process by using them as an excuse to set your sights lower. Instead, think creatively about ways to resolve possible incompatibilities.

The Six Categories of Desire

Physical Health and Well-Being: This category includes intentions related to your health, well-being, fitness, and physical development. For example, these intentions could include losing weight, feeling greater vitality, learning a sport, achieving a physical goal, or healing or reversing a disease or chronic condition.

Family and Relationships: This category includes intentions related to finding your significant other or developing an existing relationship, having or raising children, building friendships, and so on.

Money and Material Possessions: This category encompasses the material dimension of life: the wealth, abundance, and prosperity you long for and the things you dream of owning.

Career and Vocation: This category includes the success you want to achieve in business, in your professional life, or in pursuing your vocation.

Personal and Spiritual Development: This category represents the development of your heart, mind, and consciousness. It represents how you wish to grow internally. How would you like to expand your abilities and possibilities? What do you want to learn? What new skills might you develop? How do you wish to be open to possibility? How do you wish to perceive Spirit? How do you wish to raise your frequency, perceive the world, and transmit love?

Service and Contribution: This final category might include charitable or volunteer activities you want to undertake, ways you want to impact the lives of other people and the world, causes you're passionate about, and the future you want to help manifest for yourself, your loved ones, and humanity in general.

Create Your Transmitter

"In the beginning was the Word," the Bible tells us. According to Christian belief, God spoke the world into manifestation. Similarly, the Bhagavad Gita, the Hindu scripture, describes the vibratory sound "aum" or "om" as the beginning of creation. Almost every civilization throughout history has had some form or type of creation myth that involves sound. Pythagoras wrote about the "music of the spheres," a celestial vibration that most of us are not trained to hear, but that we are actually in contact with from the moment of our birth. Plato believed that the cosmos was constructed according to musical intervals and proportions. Some Native American traditions talk about the "Song of the Creator." The Hindus, Sufis, Sikhs, and Taoists all have their variations on the sound or tone that is the source of all things. The Aborigines, Aztecs, Eskimos, Malayans, and Persians have traditionally held that the Universe originated in sound. So don't underestimate the creative power of the spoken word! In this step, you use your own voice to speak the world of your dreams into manifestation.

This is the fun part. This step is where you get to create the personalized tool that will allow you to tune in to the Creation Frequency and turn your intentions into reality. Today, you don't have to use old-fashioned cassettes — you can use the phone you carry in your pocket every day. In fact, the easiest way is to use the free Creation Frequency app (see the boxed text, page 117), which is specially designed for this purpose.

Whether you use the app, your phone, your computer, or cassette tapes, here are the three steps for recording your intentions.

The Creation Frequency App

If you have a smartphone or tablet, I highly recommend that you download the Creation Frequency app. This app has been designed to make the process of recording your intentions simple and powerful. Find out more at:

TheCreationFrequency.com

Choose Your Music

It's important for your intentions to be recorded with some kind of background music that you find relaxing. Even if you have something in mind, I recommend using a particular type of music known as "theta brain wave music," since this music is attuned to the perfect frequency to put you into a trancelike state of receptivity.

Because the Intention Creation Formula is intended to reprogram your subconscious, you need to be in the optimal state to receive the vibrations of your desires. If you want to give yourself the best chance of success, I suggest choosing music that actually encourages your brain to move into a more relaxed and creatively open place.

Getting into a relaxed state isn't just about calming your emotions and your physical body — it's about shifting from one type of brain activity to another. Specifically, for the purposes of reprogramming your subconscious, you need to activate a theta state. This is because theta is the mental state in which you can consciously cocreate your reality (see the boxed text "Understanding Your Brain Wave Frequencies," pages 119–20).

Theta brain waves are related to enhanced levels of creativity in which conscious thinking is less active, while the right hemisphere is more active, with slower wave activity. As you probably know, the "right brain" is linked to emotions, images, and creativity.

In *Scientific American*, brain researcher Ned Herrmann writes that "when in theta, [people] are prone to a flow of ideas. This can also occur in the shower or tub or even while shaving or brushing your hair. It is a state where tasks become so automatic that you can mentally disengage from them."[1] In other words, in this state, you shift from the conscious to the subconscious. While alpha waves are recognized as being the "bridge" between the conscious and the subconscious, theta becomes dominant when the subconscious is fully activated. In order to become a powerful creator, you need to be able to get into that theta state, bypassing the conscious mind, and communicate directly with your subconscious.

The best way to get into a theta state is by listening to brain wave entrainment music with binaural frequencies in this range. This makes it quite easy to slip into a meditative state. While in a state of theta relaxation, you'll also experience physical benefits — your blood pressure, breathing, and heart rate will all slow to a more restful level, promoting natural healing.

The Creation Frequency app includes theta brain wave music, which has been recorded using specific frequencies for manifestation and love.

Understanding Your
Brain Wave Frequencies

Did you know that your brain has five different kinds of brain waves? Each one vibrates at a different frequency. They are known as beta, alpha, theta, delta, and gamma waves.

The **beta** wave has a frequency of 12.5 to 30 cycles per second. Beta is the state of normal waking consciousness in which you are active and alert, talking and engaging with others. It includes the functions of logic and critical reasoning.

Alpha waves have a frequency between 8 and 12.5 cycles per second. They bring about a deeply relaxed state that is associated with daydreams, as well as the transition into a state of light meditation.

The **theta** state is one of deeper relaxation, a trancelike state associated with hypnosis, meditation, and light sleep, including the REM dream state. The brain waves are slowed down at a frequency of 4 to 7 cycles per second. Some associate this state with a sense of deep spiritual connection and unity with the Universe.

Delta is the state associated with deep, dreamless sleep. Delta brain waves are the slowest of the five types, moving at a frequency between 0 and 4 cycles per second. It is also associated with very deep states of meditation, where awareness is fully detached from the conscious mind. Some people have speculated that the delta state is the gateway to the collective mind, or Jung's collective unconscious. It is also linked with deep healing and regeneration.

Only more recently discovered, **gamma** waves are the fastest brain waves. They move at above 40 Hz. While we still know very little about this state of mind, initial research indicates that gamma waves are associated with bursts of insight and high-level information processing.

Record Your Relaxation Script

Once you've chosen your music, it's time to record. The first thing you need to record is a script that will help you move into a relaxed meditative state; use the boxed text "Relaxation Script," pages 121–23. Together with the music, this simple process of physical relaxation will open the doors to the subconscious.

You may want to practice reading the script aloud a few times first so you don't stumble. Read slowly, clearly, and evenly, trying to move into the state of relaxation as you read so that the vibration of your state of being will be transmitted through the words. If you notice that you're in a stressed or anxious state, take a few minutes to breathe deeply or meditate in order to release the tension before you begin.

Relaxation Script

My breathing is slow and easy and relaxed. I inhale deeply and exhale slowly and gently...again I breathe...and again....I am so relaxed and peaceful.

I am grateful for this special moment. I am grateful for everything.

I am relaxed; my breathing is relaxed. As I gently breathe in and out, I am at peace and my mind is quiet. I am relaxed.

The muscles in my face are relaxed. My jaw muscles are relaxed. I bite down on my teeth and then release. My face and jaws are relaxed.

My neck is relaxed. I turn my neck in a circle a few times, and my neck is relaxed.

My shoulders are relaxed. I pull back and shrug my shoulders. My shoulders are relaxed.

I am so very relaxed. My breathing is so gentle, natural, and relaxed.

My arms are relaxed. Hanging gently from my shoulders, my arms are relaxed.

My hands are relaxed. I squeeze my hands into fists tightly and then release the grip. My hands are relaxed.

I am relaxed. I breathe gently in and out, and I love the sensation. I am grateful for the gift of breath.

My stomach muscles are relaxed. I tighten them and then release them. My stomach is relaxed.

My butt muscles are relaxed. I tighten them and release them. My buttocks are relaxed. I am relaxed.

My hamstrings are relaxed. I tighten them and then release them. My hamstrings are relaxed; I am relaxed.

My hips are relaxed. My blood flows through my hip joints, healing my joints and bringing me peace. My hips are open and relaxed.

My thighs are relaxed. I am relaxed.

My knees work perfectly. My knees are relaxed; my knees serve me.

I am relaxed. My breathing is relaxed, and I am at peace.

I am so very grateful. I love myself and everything in my life. I am love, and I am relaxed.

My calves are relaxed. I stretch my calves, and my calves are relaxed.

My ankles are relaxed. I move my ankles in circles, and my ankles are relaxed. I am relaxed.

I am at deep peace, and I am relaxed.

My feet are relaxed. My feet ground me to Mother Earth, and my feet are very relaxed. I wiggle my toes. My toes are relaxed.

I am relaxed and in a deep and grateful space. I am one with all, one with the energy of the Universe.

I am all-powerful. I am love, I am peace, and I am free to create my heart's desire.

I am relaxed.

I am.

Read Your Intentions

Once you've recorded the relaxation script, it's time to record your intentions. As you read each one, try to put yourself emotionally in the state of consciousness you're describing. It may take a few tries before you are really tuned in. If you've written your intentions in the way I suggest, they will be full of feeling, which you will transmit through your voice. Read with passion and conviction, slowly, clearly, and purposefully. When you finish each intention, pause for a few seconds and allow the music to play before you read the next intention.

Congratulations: You've just created your own personal Creation Frequency transmitter, a tool that will enable you to become a powerful creator.

Listen with Your Subconscious

In order for this tool to work, you need to be in a state of deep relaxation. The best times for this are right before you go to sleep at night and just after you wake up in the morning, when your brain is naturally in a theta state. This is the optimal time to listen to your recorded intentions.

Start by sitting quietly and connecting with your deeper self in whatever way you choose. Once you are focused on that vibration of inner wisdom, turn on your relaxation script recording and follow its instructions. Let your body unwind one part at a time, from your face down through your neck and to the tips of your fingers and toes. Breathe deeply and peacefully, filling yourself up with love and gratitude. This process, together with the music, will move you into a deeper state of physical and mental ease in which your subconscious is much more receptive.

Once you are in a state of deep relaxation, though not sleeping, play your recorded intentions. Breathe deeply as you listen, as this will continue to attune your personal vibration to the music and the energetic quality of your intentions. Keep your mind relaxed — this is not the time to plan or figure out how to achieve your intentions. Just absorb the vibration of the words and the emotions, and breathe out your love and gratitude to the Universe.

In addition to listening to the intentions morning and night, as many times as you want, you may want to play them at other times, such as when you are driving in the car or taking a walk. Interestingly, brain researchers say that driving is one of the activities that can move us into a theta state because it is a skill we perform unconsciously.

You may also want to try putting your recorded intentions on repeat and allowing them to play while you fall asleep and through the night. If you sleep with a partner, you will need headphones for this, of course. As you move through the theta state of REM sleep into the delta state of deep sleep, perhaps your intentions will imprint themselves even more deeply upon your subconscious and connect to the universal consciousness.

What is happening as you are listening? The frequencies of your emotionally powerful and clearly proclaimed intentions reprogram your subconscious mind to be a more loving, powerful reflection of who you truly are. They remove the limiting beliefs of the past and align you with the new reality of your intentions. Once your subconscious mind and your heart are aligned, the frequency of your intentions, combined with your heart and mind energy, goes out in waves into the Universe, reorganizing the atoms of the Universe to shift reality.

Enjoy Yourself!

Are you ready to start communicating your desires to the Universe using your personal transmitter? It may sound implausible that such a simple tool has the power to change your life forever. I must admit, all those years ago, when the mystery man handed me my cassette tape, I had my fair share of doubts. But by that point, I'd invested so much in this process that I firmly pushed them aside, ready to do exactly as he had instructed.

"Our work together is done," he said, as he walked with me to the door, putting his hand on my shoulder. "Go home and transmit your intentions to the Universe, and have no doubt that you are already moving toward the life you truly want. As your desires begin to manifest, you will become aware of new, creative solutions and possibilities. Stay attuned, listen to the messages you are receiving as well as those you are transmitting. Be ready to adapt and upgrade your intentions as you go. And remember, whatever you do, enjoy yourself! Why waste any of your precious time doing less than what brings you alive?"

8

Promises Fulfilled

LIVING IN TUNE WITH THE CREATION FREQUENCY

God is a frequency. Stay tuned.
— Alan Cohen

When I drove away from the mystery man's house after my last session, I was resolved: I would follow his instructions to the letter. In fact, I popped the cassette into the car stereo and began listening immediately (driving is a great time to transmit your intentions!). Every morning and every night, I listened to that cassette. And it worked — beyond anything I could have imagined.

Did my dreams come true overnight? No, it took time. But I persisted. After two years my first and most important intention began to manifest. Remember, I was estranged from my wife and baby daughter. It would have been understandable if she had never wanted to see me again — she'd divorced me for good reason. And yet, one day, she called me up out of th

to go with her to a Christmas party

reconciled, and we went on to rem

and have three more wonderful chil

My next intention had been to o

Because I already worked in the ree

natural inclination was to open a r

have any money to get started. E

that intention describing the wond

own, and I also remembered the m

listen to the messages the Univers

attention to your intuition, and be p

of nowhere, an idea occurred to me

the paper asking for investors. So

no cash, no credit, and a negative

to raise enough money to open m

year of setting that intention. I ha

ness almost ever since.

I'd also set an intention to ear

the years following my meetings

my income rose steadily, soon su

reaching as high as $300,000 a mo

blessed with a life of wealth and

have been unimaginable to my yo

Next came my home — that I

visioned for my family, with an

none of the fear that had marred

Soon after my wife and I ren

buy a beautiful house with no do

8

Promises Fulfilled

LIVING IN TUNE WITH
THE CREATION FREQUENCY

God is a frequency. Stay tuned.
— Alan Cohen

When I drove away from the mystery man's house after my last session, I was resolved: I would follow his instructions to the letter. In fact, I popped the cassette into the car stereo and began listening immediately (driving is a great time to transmit your intentions!). Every morning and every night, I listened to that cassette. And it worked — beyond anything I could have imagined.

Did my dreams come true overnight? No, it took time. But I persisted. After two years my first and most important intention began to manifest. Remember, I was estranged from my wife and baby daughter. It would have been understandable if she had never wanted to see me again — she'd divorced me for good reason. And yet, one day, she called me up out of the blue and asked me to go with her to a Christmas party. Soon after, we were reconciled, and we went on to remarry six months later and have three more wonderful children.

My next intention had been to own my own business. Because I already worked in the restaurant industry, my natural inclination was to open a restaurant, but I didn't have any money to get started. Every day, I listened to that intention describing the wonderful business I would own, and I also remembered the mystery man's advice — listen to the messages the Universe is sending you. Pay attention to your intuition, and be proactive. One day, out of nowhere, an idea occurred to me. I should put an ad in the paper asking for investors. So I did. Despite having no cash, no credit, and a negative net worth, I was able to raise enough money to open my own business within a year of setting that intention. I have owned my own business almost ever since.

I'd also set an intention to earn $10,000 a month. In the years following my meetings with the mystery man, my income rose steadily, soon surpassing my goal and reaching as high as $300,000 a month at times. I have been blessed with a life of wealth and abundance that would have been unimaginable to my younger self.

Next came my home — that love-filled haven I'd envisioned for my family, with an always-open door and none of the fear that had marred my own childhood.

Soon after my wife and I remarried, we were able to buy a beautiful house with no down payment, and I have since owned even more palatial residences in some of my favorite places in the country.

I also enjoyed great health, as I'd envisioned in my fifth intention, despite my earlier abuses on my body with drink and drugs.

In short, I got everything I asked for. But I'll be honest with you: Something was still missing. Later, I would come to understand that I'd neglected the most important of my intentions — the intention to help disadvantaged young people.

Although I once taught a course at a juvenile hall, and I made time to coach little league baseball and to give the occasional speech at my local church, I lost sight of the only one of my desires that represented something I would give, not something I wanted for myself. I was distracted by all of the wonderful things that were manifesting in my life.

It took many years, and a painful loss, before I reconnected with that feeling of compassion that the mystery man had described. The intention took a different form than I had originally envisioned — helping people with cancer — but serving others finally manifested and has become the central theme of my life. Under the auspices of my foundation, I have also helped several young men who were struggling with the demons of addiction, which had tormented me as a teenager. At those moments, I have felt a particular fulfillment in seeing the intention I'd put out into the Universe decades before come full circle.

I hope you can avoid my mistake and keep the element of compassion and service alive throughout the process. As your dreams start to come true, as you get the things you've always wanted and achieve the goals you set for yourself, don't just sit back and tune out again. If you do, the frequency you are transmitting will gradually slip down the scale, and your power and connection to the cosmic forces will weaken. The challenge for the master creator is to keep raising your personal frequency. Love and compassion are the guaranteed shortcut to doing so.

Remember Penney Peirce's emotional frequencies chart (see "The Scales of Everyday Vibrations" on page 62)? At the top of that chart are love and empathy. Generosity is also close to the top. These emotions point us toward the most powerful thing we can do to raise our personal frequency: *give*. Service and contribution — which mean giving to others — are, paradoxically, the key to creating more and more of what you want in this life. Once again, giving should not be an afterthought — it should be woven into every step of your journey because it is the missing piece that will bring you true happiness and amplify the love in the Universe.

Think of the Creation Frequency as being like an electrical circuit — a virtuous circuit of cocreation, a circle of love. There is a circular flow between our own frequency and the universal frequency, between giving and receiving, that continually amplifies itself and raises its vibrations. In the activation of this circuit, we are given an even greater gift than the fulfillment of our desires —

we are given the opportunity to give back. We have the opportunity both to manifest the life of our dreams and to help others find theirs as well.

I experience an unquenchable desire to help others and to share whatever love and support I am able to provide. I have noticed that as soon as this momentum of giving is set into motion within my heart, magic begins happening in my life on a daily basis. The right people start to appear just when I need them, resources become abundant, and situations that would once have been difficult to navigate begin to flow effortlessly. It really does seem as if the stars begin to align.

This is why I believe that the purpose of life is to serve. That is what will raise your personal vibration to the highest level and supercharge your creative powers. Start today, right now, with an open and compassionate heart. Give love, give kindness, give a smile, or simply give your attention. It will come back to you a hundredfold.

Be Open to Receive Your Dreams in Whatever Shape They Come

Remember, although you've taken the time to envision your desires and to describe them with emotional power and authenticity, they may not always show up in the form you expect. I recently met a young woman named Karen who said that her most cherished dream had been to have a child. She wrote this as one of her intentions, infusing it with love and longing for this unborn child, whom she imagined as a beautiful baby with her same green eyes. At the time, Karen was single. While she was willing to have a child alone, she hoped to meet a man with whom to share this dream, which was another intention she developed. Then she met Lewis, who was tall, handsome, funny — and the widowed father of two young boys. When Lewis proposed, Karen became not just a wife but a mother. "I thought long and hard about that baby I'd envisioned," she said. "Was I still supposed to have it? Or was this the fulfillment of my intention in a different form?" Ultimately, Karen decided that two young sons more than satisfied her desire for motherhood. She loves the boys as if they were her own, and whenever she looks into their blue eyes, she sees the reflection of the man she loves.

Be open to receive your dreams in whatever form they appear. Trust that sometimes the Universe knows better than you. Don't be too quick to say no to opportunities and gifts just because they don't look like what you thought you wanted. At moments like this, try to tune in to the "feeling" quality of your intention rather than the specifics, and ask: Does this new direction carry the same emotional vibration even if it doesn't look the way I thought it would look? If it is emotionally aligned and attuned with the vibrations of your original statement, chances are it will be the right thing.

Although you are channeling all of your energy toward the realization of your desires, it is important to be open-minded and ready to let go. This may sound contradictory, but as the saying goes, the opposite of a great truth is another great truth. Surrender and acceptance are as critical to the flow of energy in the Universe as intention and creativity. Trust that the Universe will deliver what you need, even if it doesn't look the way you think it should.

Also, be open to the fact that life will sometimes throw you a curveball, and even the best-laid plans and the most carefully attuned intentions can't stand up to the onslaught of reality. I believe deeply in the power of the human mind to cocreate its own reality — and I think most of us underestimate this power. But I also believe that we live in a Universe that we can't always understand or control. I don't see that Universe as random and meaningless; in fact, I think it is guided by a much greater intelligence than ours. But this intelligence doesn't always reveal its workings to us. Through tapping into the Creation Frequency, you can certainly learn to become more attuned to that intelligence and to work with it. Sometimes you'll feel like "the Universe is on my side!" But other times the Universe may simply have different plans for you.

Ongoing monitoring, measuring, and adjusting is an integral part of the creation process. Life is moving and changing all the time, so you need to be awake and continually realigning yourself to it. Imagine you are a pilot flying a plane to Hawaii. Once you reach your cruising altitude, you can relax and sit back for a while, but you need to stay alert. You may notice that the wind is pushing the plane a little off track, or some unexpected turbulence might make it advisable to fly higher. It's up to you to make these and countless other small adjustments to keep the plane on course to its destination. In the same way, as you move toward your intentions, you will need to monitor, measure, and adjust constantly.

At a certain point in my own journey, after I had owned my own restaurant for some time, I had to adjust my business intention. A buddy of mine was working in the car business, and I couldn't help but notice that he was making a lot more money than I was making in the restaurant business. So I changed my intention — and since then I have owned several thriving car dealerships.

As you become attuned to the Universe's messages, you'll start to know when to stay the course, when to make small adjustments, and when you've encountered one of those rare instances where you need to change direction completely.

Remember, this is a *co*creative process, and as such, it requires that you work together with the Universe. As you work on transmitting your intentions, stay attuned to the messages you're receiving back. Are you consistently getting signals that perhaps you're on the wrong path? Has something unplanned come into your life — like a new opportunity, a new person, or an unexpected ending? I like the saying "when one door closes, another door opens." This is how the Universe works.

For example, perhaps one of your intentions was to

build your business to a certain size, but then, out of the blue, an offer to buy the business appears. At a moment like this, you may need to go back and connect with your deeper self, tuning in to what might be possible if you were to accept the offer. What other dreams might that money enable you to fulfill? What might be the hidden costs? If you decide to change course, take the time to develop a new intention to replace the one you are letting go of.

Sometimes the unexpected comes in the form of a setback. Perhaps your intention is to run a marathon, and you suddenly get sick or become injured. Again, reconnect with your inner wisdom and inquire: *Is this a temporary setback that I need to overcome, or is it a message from the Universe telling me I need to slow down and take care of myself in other ways?*

Sometimes the Universe tests us. Other times it redirects us. Only you can discern which is which. If your spiritual intention is to find more inner peace, you may find yourself overwhelmed with fears, anxieties, or out-of-control thoughts racing through your mind every time you sit down to meditate. It may feel like you are getting further away from your goal, not closer, and the temptation may be overwhelming: *Why am I sitting here like this? I'd be more peaceful just knocking back a couple of beers and turning on the TV. Heck, I'd be more peaceful going to sleep.* But if you persevere, you may discover that true spiritual peace is not simply a nice feeling or the absence of uncomfortable thoughts and disturbances. It's a place deep within where you can rest even when your mind is moving a million miles an hour. If you can pass the test of those difficult times without giving up, you'll gain access to a gift that is precious beyond measure.

Give It Time

A final piece of advice: Give it time. Don't expect your desires to manifest overnight. This process is not magic — it's habit change. The kind of habits you are working with are not physical actions like quitting smoking or taking a walk every day — they are subconscious patterns of thought and feeling that you are seeking to replace with new, intentional patterns. So be patient and realistic. Give yourself time and stick with it.

If you read popular motivational books, you may have heard that it takes twenty-one days, or thirty days, to change a habit. However, researchers from University College London did a study that indicates that it might take quite a lot longer than that. The study asked participants to choose one new habit to adopt over a twelve-week period. These were simple habits, like taking a daily run or drinking a bottle of water. Each day, the participants reported whether they did the new behavior and whether it felt automatic. In their analysis of the data, the research team wanted to shed light on how long it took each person to go from starting a new behavior to when it became a habit. What they found was that, on average, it took sixty-six days.[1] And remember, these were much simpler habits than the kind we're talking about. So don't be discouraged or passive if your intentions take longer to materialize than you would like. It may take many years for your intentions to manifest — especially the big ones.

Enjoy Yourself

Finally, remember the mystery man's parting words to me: Enjoy yourself! It's the journey that gives life juice, not the destination. Look for every opportunity to cocreate the life you desire with the Universe. Don't just sit and wait — take action! As you train your subconscious on your intentions by using this process, it will start channeling key pieces of information to your conscious mind. You will start to see the plans and strategies that will allow you to manifest your goals. For example, when I expressed my intention to own my own business, it suddenly became clear that I should put an ad in the paper to seek investors. By doing so, I got the funding that allowed me to take the first critical steps toward my dream.

Listen to your intentions at least twice a day. If you have been practicing the steps in this book, you are well on your way to becoming a powerful creator. Have faith in yourself and in the process. Because I believe wholeheartedly in my intentions, they manifest. Things just show up in my life, seemingly effortlessly. As you progress and you see your intentions manifest, you will come to understand that everything you speak is recorded in the memory of the Universe and reverberates infinitely. What you proclaim will come to be.

Epilogue

A MYSTERY SOLVED

It's a strange feeling to owe all of the most important things in your life to someone whose name you cannot recall. As I worked on this book, more and more memories surfaced of my seven weeks with the mystery man, but his identity still eluded me. Finally, I reconnected with the friend who had originally introduced me to him, and he gave me a name.

Doug Fitzgerald.

I typed it into Google but nothing much came up. Determined to track down this man who had made such a difference in my life, I hired a private investigator and told him what little I knew. Several weeks later, I began to get answers to my questions.

Sadly, I learned that Douglas Preston Fitzgerald passed away in 2011. It is one of my great regrets that I did not begin my search sooner and have the opportunity to sit down with him one more time at the kitchen table and tell him how every one of those intentions we wrote came true. I did, however, connect with his son, and thus I learned more about the life and work of the guy I've always thought of as the mystery man.

Doug was born in 1930 in Boone, Iowa. With an IQ of 180, he was a member of Mensa, but he struggled with college. As a young man, like me, he tended to run from his problems, so he hitchhiked to California and joined the navy. He worked many different jobs, mostly in sales, and succumbed to alcoholism in his twenties, which he would struggle with for several decades. When I met him, in the early eighties, he'd gone through AA and got sober, and he'd begun to dedicate himself to helping others recover.

Doug read and studied much of the leading-edge literature of the time on personal growth, human potential, and spirituality, including the writings of Buckminster Fuller and the Silva Mind Control method. His son told me that he loved nothing more than helping people. He identified the values that guided him as love, compassion, wisdom, caring, and service.

In the second half of his life, Doug worked with thousands of people in recovery programs and business programs that he designed himself, based on the most effective methods he'd learned. I was but one of many beneficiaries of this unusual man's wisdom and insight.

In 2001, Doug suffered a massive stroke. His doctors said he would not survive the night, but he went on to live ten more years. He and his wife, Geraldine, had four children, who were very touched to hear my memories of their father, and they were gracious in sharing his story and his writings with me for this book.

I will end with a few of Doug's words, written to his children at the age of sixty-five, shortly before his stroke. His theme was hope.

Hope is necessary to play the life game joyously. What could I hope for at this age? I could hope for harmony, for love, for acceptance, for balance, for flexibility, for wisdom, for compassion, for abundance.

There is enough sorrow. I don't need to add more to the world. There are enough causes for all who want to live in sorrow and fight joy.

But I will fight for joy. It is not automatic. It needs to be practiced. Joy comes from the heart, mind, and soul coming together in a powerful recognition of our true state — our aliveness. To be alive is a rowdy affair, thrashing around for expression like a child in a leaf pile.

Watch your children before you corrupt them. Watch them play, explore, risk, and explode in a rush of energy as they experience the blessed moment fully. No analysis, no history, no rules, just focused energy sensing their total environment in partnership with their play.

See your sad faces, your evening news, your cause-oriented issues. You have failed as a society that knows how to produce joy....

I weep not for a society that might have been. You are entitled to your sorrow — stay with it if you wish. I choose joy, to continue loving, playing, and experiencing it in the blessed moment of the now.

Douglas Preston Fitzgerald, circa 1989

ACKNOWLEDGMENTS

What can I say about the guy who literally pulled my
life out of the gutter and taught me the art of manifestation? By using and embracing his technique, I created a
life of such abundance that even after all of these years it
still astounds me. I've never encountered anything as effective as the process he taught me, before or since. Once
we understand this technique, we can literally create anything we deeply desire. Thank you, Doug Fitzgerald,
a.k.a. the mystery man.

And to my friend of thirty-five years, Dave Casteel,
thank you so much for introducing me to Mr. Fitzgerald.

My gratitude also extends to Doug Fitzgerald's family — in particular, his son Michael — for graciously re-
sponding to my inquiries after I finally tracked down the
identity of the man who had helped me so much three decades ago. Thank you for taking the time to tell me about
your late father and sharing his memories and writings.

To my dear friend and mentor Marcia Wieder, thank
you so much for encouraging me to get this book out
there and for helping me name it *The Creation Frequency*!

To all the authors who have written about or taught the laws of attraction, manifestation, and intentions, thank you. It was your work that sustained me whenever any fear-based mental noise crept in. Whenever I doubted that my diligence in listening daily to my intentions would bear fruit, your writings inspired me and kept me steadfast on the path. I am especially grateful that one of my favorite authors, Penney Peirce, agreed to write the preface for this book. When I first met Jack Canfield, I told him that after reading *The Success Principles*, I'd felt disheartened — I wondered if there was still a book for me to write, since he seemed to have said everything I wanted to say, and more. However, I persevered in telling my story, and I am honored that Jack himself has graciously provided a foreword.

And last but definitely not least, a special thanks to the cocreator of all my books, Ellen Daly. I am more of a storyteller, a guy who likes to take big concepts and make them simple, but Ellen is truly a gifted writer, capable of sitting with me and listening to my stories, concepts, and ideas and then turning them into a beautiful book. Thank you, Ellen!

NOTES

1. Why You're Not Already Living the Life of Your Dreams: Week One

1. Prentice Mulford, *Thoughts Are Things* (London: Thinking Ink Media, 2011), 116.
2. Jack Canfield, "Using the Law of Attraction for Joy, Relationships, Money & More," Canfield Training Group, accessed October 2017, http://jackcanfield.com/blog/using-the-law-of-attraction.
3. "Latest Happiness Index Reveals American Happiness at All-Time Low," Harris Poll, last updated July 8, 2016, http://www.theharrispoll.com/health-and-life/American-Happiness-at-All-Time-Low.html.
4. AARP survey cited in Stephen Marche, "Is Facebook Making Us Lonely?" *The Atlantic*, May 2012, accessed June 2016, http://www.theatlantic.com/magazine/archive/2012/05/is-facebook-making-us-lonely/308930.
5. Peter Wehrwein, "Astounding Increase in Antidepressant Use by Americans," *Harvard Health Blog*, October 20, 2011, http://www.health.harvard.edu/blog/astounding

-increase-in-antidepressant-use-by-americans-2011
10203624.

6. Bruce Lipton, *Spontaneous Evolution* (Carlsbad, CA: Hay House, 2010), 12.

7. David Eagleman, *Incognito: The Secret Lives of the Brain* (New York: Random House, 2011), 140–41.

8. Joseph Murphy, *The Power of Your Subconscious Mind* (Englewood Cliffs, NJ: Prentice-Hall, 1963), 76.

9. Gregg Braden, *The Spontaneous Healing of Belief: Shattering the Paradigm of False Limits* (Carlsbad, CA: Hay House, 2009), iii.

10. Wayne Dyer, from a talk at Wanderlust California Yoga Festival, July 2012, reported in *Wanderlust Journal*, April 19, 2013, https://wanderlust.com/journal/wayne -dyer-master-art-manifesting/ (accessed February 7, 2018).

2. The Intention Creation Formula: Week Two

1. Danielle LaPorte, *The Desire Map: A Guide to Creating Goals with Soul* (Louisville, CO: Sounds True, 2014), 7–11.

2. Mark Epstein, *Open to Desire: The Truth about What the Buddha Taught* (New York: Penguin, 2008), 8.

3. Marcia Wieder, *Dream: Clarify and Create What You Want* (Las Vegas: Next Century Publishing, 2016), 94.

3. How the Universe Really Works: Week Three

1. Donald Hatch Andrews, quoted in Don Campbell, *Music: Physician for Times to Come* (Wheaton, IL: Quest Books, 2014), 288.

2. Niels Bohr, *The Philosophical Writings of Niels Bohr, Vol. 3: Essays 1958–1962 on Atomic Physics and Human Knowledge* (Woodbridge, CT: Ox Bow Press, 1995).

3. Richard Feynman, *The Character of Physical Law* (New York: Modern Library, 1994), 129.

4. Albert Einstein, quoted in the film *Atomic Physics* (United World Films, J. Arthur Rank Organization, Ltd., 1948), from the National Archives Catalog, https://catalog .archives.gov/id/88106.

5. Max Planck, acceptance speech for the 1918 Nobel Prize for Physics, quoted in Clifford Pickover, *Archimedes to Hawking: Laws of Science and the Great Minds Behind Them* (New York: Oxford University Press, 2008), 417.

6. Lynne McTaggart, *The Field: The Quest for the Secret Force of the Universe* (New York: Harper Perennial, 2008), 19.

7. Wendy Doniger, trans., *The Rig Veda* (London: Penguin UK, 2005).

8. Fritjof Capra, *The Tao of Physics* (Boulder, CO: Shambhala Publications, 2010), 19.

9. Ibid., 11.

10. Werner Heisenberg, *Physics and Philosophy: The Revolution in Modern Science* (New York: Harper Perennial, 2007), 186.

11. Lynne McTaggart, *The Intention Experiment: Using Your Thoughts to Change Your Life and the World* (New York: Atria Books, 2008), xxii–xxiii.

12. Lynne McTaggart, *The Field*, 11–12.

13. Ibid., xxiii.

14. Planck, 1918 Nobel Prize acceptance speech, quoted in Pickover, *Archimedes to Hawking*, 417.

15. Eckhart Tolle, *The Power of Now: A Guide to Spiritual Enlightenment* (Novato, CA: New World Library, 2004), 111.

16. Deepak Chopra, *The Seven Spiritual Laws of Success: A Practical Guide to the Fulfillment of Your Dreams* (Novato, CA: New World Library/Amber-Allen Publishing, 1994), 1.

17. Penney Peirce, *Frequency: The Power of Personal Vibration* (New York: Atria Books/Beyond Words, 2011), 27.

18. Masaru Emoto, *The Hidden Messages in Water* (New York: Atria Books, 2011), 39.

19. Ibid., 44.

20. R. H. Jarrett, *It Works: The Famous Little Red Book That Makes Your Dreams Come True!* (New York: DeVorss & Company, 1992), 4.

21. Na Cai et al., "Molecular Signatures of Major Depression," *Current Biology* 25, no. 9 (May 4, 2015): 1146–56, http://www.cell.com/current-biology/abstract/S0960 -9822(15)00322-X.

22. HeartMath Institute, "You Can Change Your DNA," July 14, 2011, https://www.heartmath.org/articles-of -the-heart/personal-development/you-can-change -your-dna.

4. From Fear to Love: Week Four

1. Neale Donald Walsch, *Communion with God* (New York: TarcherPerigee, 2002), 71.

2. Gerald G. Jampolsky, *Love Is Letting Go of Fear* (New York: Celestial Arts, 2010), 47.

3. Charles F. Haanel, *The Master Key System* (New York: SoHo Books, 2013), 58.

4. Ibid., 79–80.

5. Dante Alighieri, *Divine Comedy, Longfellow's Translation, Complete* (Los Angeles: HardPress Publishing, 2010), 496.

6. Daniel Pinchbeck, "The universe only pretends to be made of matter. Secretly, it is made of love." *Twitter*, February 23, 2012, https://twitter.com/danielpinchbeck/status/172950055752445952.

7. Brian Swimme, *The Universe Is a Green Dragon: A Cosmic Creation Story* (Rochester, NY: Bear & Company, 1994).

8. Ibid.

5. Raise Your Frequency: Week Five

1. Deepak Chopra, *The Spontaneous Fulfillment of Desire: Harnessing the Infinite Power of Coincidence* (New York: Harmony/Random House, 2003), 21.

6. The Power of Giving: Week Six

1. Lynne Twist, *The Soul of Money* (New York: W. W. Norton, 2006), 8.

2. Rosabeth Moss Kanter, "The Happiest People Pursue the Most Difficult Problems," *Harvard Business Review Blog Network*, April 10, 2013, http://blogs.hbr.org/kanter/2013/04/to-find-happiness-at-work-tap.html.

3. Viktor Frankl, *Man's Search for Ultimate Meaning* (New York: Basic Books, 2000), 90.

4. Viktor Frankl, *Man's Search for Meaning* (New York: Beacon Press, 2006), 88.

5. Ibid., 12.

7. The Mystery Man's Gift: Week Seven

1. Ned Herrmann, "What Is the Function of the Various Brainwaves?" *Scientific American*, December 22, 1997, http://www.scientificamerican.com/article/what-is -the-function-of-t-1997-12-22.

8: Promises Fulfilled: Living in Tune with the Creation Frequency

1. Phillippa Lally et al., "How Are Habits Formed: Modelling Habit Formation in the Real World," *European Journal of Social Psychology* 40, no. 6 (October 2010): 998–1009, doi:10.1002/ejsp.674.

For further resources, tools, support,
and inspiration, visit:

MikeMurphyUnfiltered.com

All net proceeds from royalties and course sales
go to support low-income women with cancer
through the Love from Margot Foundation.

ABOUT THE AUTHOR

Mike Murphy is a successful entrepreneur, speaker, coach, and philanthropist. His mission is to share exactly how he has been able to cocreate a life of extraordinary freedom, abundance, purpose, and love.

Mike is the president and owner of Volkswagen of Oakland in Oakland, California, a role he has held since 1996. He is the founder of the Love from Margot Foundation, which he established in honor of his late wife, who lived with cancer courageously for nine years. The foundation supports low-income women experiencing advanced cancer by providing them with emergency funds, education, and resources needed for recovery. He is also the founder of Mountains of Hope, a transformational retreat center in Colombia, South America, dedicated to delivering cutting-edge healing modalities to those who suffer from cancer, addiction, and disconnectedness from life. In addition, through his *Creation Frequency* online course, he coaches people in creating the lives of their dreams. His first book, *Love Unfiltered*, was a *Wall Street Journal* bestseller.

TheCreationFrequency.com